THE KEY CLASS

The Keys to Job Search Success

Volume I

John J. Daly, Jr.

Troll River Publications

www.trollriverpub.com

Presents

The Key Class

The Keys to Job Search Success

www.thekeyclass.com

For information, contact johnkeyclass@gmail.com or

www.thekeyclass.com

Table of Contents

Contents

AUTHOR'S PERSONAL NOTE

When I work with students today, many of them despair because they don't know how they can better their life situations. I met such a young man recently, and he really didn't want to participate in The Key Class until I told him this story. I share it with you in hopes that it will encourage you to reach further, try harder and fill your purpose with determination.

I was born into a middle-class family and raised by my mother after she and my dad divorced when I was 18 months old. My mother became the very successful president of a construction company in upstate New York. We lived the high life (so to speak) until I was 9 years old, when we lost everything, and I mean everything.

In 1957, my mother took my older brother and me to Miami, Florida, where we settled in a black ghetto. My mother found a job on the other side of town, but we were so poor that she had no money for bus fare or any other type of transportation to and from work. My brother managed to get a bike and would take my mom to work on the crossbar of the bike every day and then go on to school. Then, he would pick her up after school and bring her home. My job at age 10 was to keep the house clean and have dinner ready for the family when they got home.

It was during these times that I decided I would never allow this to happen to any of us again.

I'd like to say that I overcame our situation because I excelled at education, but I was never a good student, primarily because I was unable to concentrate on the tasks at hand. By today's standards, I would have been diagnosed with ADD. But I worked hard to get passing grades and loved being in school for the social life it provided.

We slowly managed to find our way out of this mess; we all pitched in as a team and overcame each challenge. We moved to Los Angeles when I was 13 years old and bought a new home. We were finally doing well again! Unbelievably, I graduated from high school in the top third of the class, only because I worked very hard to make it happen. I didn't go to college. In reality, I had taken my first job when I was 8 years old in New York and have worked every day since.

At age 18, I miraculously started working in the event industry, before it was formalized as it has been today. From my life in poverty, I was highly motivated to start my own business and be in control! After I launched my business, my average work day was a minimum of 15 hours, sometimes 20. If it was 10 hours, I considered it a short day. But the hours didn't matter. I loved what I was doing, so it was easy for me to work until my tasks for the day were completed.

Fortunately, I was at the right place at the right time with the right attitude, and my business became very successful. It grew into an international company. At one time, I owned six different businesses. After moving to

Santa Barbara in the early '90s, I bought my family an estate behind gates in Montecito through my hard work.

How? *Hard work and dedication* to my field. I have always treated everyone in business with the greatest respect and have worked with a very high code of ethics. Always considering the comfort of others and using correct business manners brought me full circle to a life of which I am proud.

I have retired from the wonderful industry of events and have turned to teaching job readiness skills to high school students and young adults up to 30 years old. Because business etiquette was a large part of my success, it's important for me to share it with others at a time when it is critical for them to learn it.

The life lesson that has meant the most to me and the one I want to share with you is simply: "It is not about what happens to you but how you react to it that determines your path and final destination."

Neither my mother, my brother, nor I had to go back to a ghetto, ever. For that, I am truly grateful.

INTRODUCTION

Why Etiquette?

Why not? Did you know that 70 percent of people lose their jobs because they don't fit into the work environment? It has become even more difficult to get a job. When I explain to people that the reason they aren't appearing to "fit in" leads back to their not understanding business and personal etiquette, I'm met with, "You mean that stuffy, eat-with-the-right-fork stuff?"

Far from it. Think of job hunting as *a game.* Job hunting depends on knowing the rules of the game. Like playing a game of football, you need to know all the rules, particularly the ones you don't want to break, such as being out-of-bounds.

The point of the game in job searching *and* in life is to *know how to be comfortable and make others comfortable with you in every situation.* And that's *why etiquette!*

So, why are so many people lacking in an understanding of the rules? My response is simple: No one has ever taught them!

Over the past several years, I've been mentoring young people and coaching at-risk teens through the Teen Court in Santa Barbara, California. In the process, I launched The Key Class, a course on business and social manners to help these students secure jobs and gain college entrance. Initially, I was amazed at how many of my students didn't know how to shake hands properly, dress correctly for an interview, eat a meal with appropriate table manners, write a thank you note or even look others in the eye when having a conversation with them.

Here's an extreme example that was a shocking realization for me. I had just begun to mentor a young, at-risk teen. Our first time having a meal together was a real eye-opener. He ordered chili and began to eat it with his hands! I was still walking on egg shells, so to speak, and had to be very careful how I behaved with him. So, I said, "I know that this is our first time out together having a meal, but this just won't work for me. I would like to help you with a few things that I think you need to learn, so please go into the restroom and wash your hands."

While he was in the restroom, I supplied his side of the table with a napkin and the proper utensils. When he came back to the table, I told him to unfold the napkin and put it in his lap. Then I showed him how to hold his spoon correctly and eat his food. He really was very grateful by the time we finished the meal. He admitted to me that he had no idea how to behave when dining in public. I was just grateful not to have to watch him eat with his hands any longer, but this incident drove home that our young people aren't always being taught the social manners critical to their long-term success!

This book is a compilation of articles I've written over the past few years. I've even snagged a few guest bloggers along the way. The book, along with a companion guide, illustrates how to create and maintain a great first impression, and why that's important. It includes how to handle greetings and introductions; tips for job interviews and how to follow up; how to make the dreaded small talk; how to listen; dressing for success (even on a budget); proper table manners; the problem with cell phones, email and social media; how to conduct yourself at work to get ahead; some great rules of thumb to follow in both your business and social life; and more!

Get ready to download a winning formula for success!

WHY GOOD MANNERS MATTER

The X Factor

Simon Cowell brought the highly successful *X Factor* hit U.K. show to the U.S. with rave reviews. But just what is the X Factor? In TV-land, is it 13-year-old Diamond White's vulnerability or 2012 winner Tate Stevens' amazing likeability? From what I can tell, the judges on the show are really looking for a personality or performance element that is unique, yes . . . but also a quality that connects with something in the popular culture that appeals to the audience.

In one of his blogs, Larry Comp, a principal business consultant at LTC Performance, asks how the X Factor applies in the business context and how it relates to choosing and developing top-performing employees. The question motivated me to ask Facebook and Twitter friends the following:

1. What is the X Factor that you see in your top performers?
2. What makes the most valuable members of your team really stand out?

My long-time friend Andrea Michaels of Extraordinary Events gave me the best answer. She wrote:

"The X Factor is that internal need to give more than what is being asked for because they have no choice in the matter . . . It's just who they are. Before you can ask them to do something, they've already done it because they want to. It's not about scoring points. It's about what they *need* to do . . . which is shine, just because they want to and deserve to do so and it's who they are. Making sense? And always with graciousness and enthusiasm with no clock-watching. It's like kids in school who take more classes than they need to just for the joy of learning."

Superstars in entertainment or business have that unexplainable or unique quality that makes them sparkle and seem appealing to others. In business, they apply their special something in a way that really resonates in their organization's culture and adds extra value in working toward its specific goals. They've figured out how to marry their unique strengths with the needs of the business and the culture of the organization. Those who achieve this combination usually care about other people and are gracious and respectful.

This leads me back to my favorite topic—good manners. In today's world, good manners and respectful behavior will set you apart from the pack. Simon Cowell may have built his success on his seemingly rude behavior, but a lasting superstar's X Factor secret ingredient is knowing how to treat others the right way.

A Keen Eye

A Facebook friend and associate, Ruth Moyte, asked this morning if we knew the definition of "perspicacious." It's having or showing an ability to notice and understand things that are difficult or not obvious. It's a synonym for "keen."

I've often wondered why I have such a keen perspective on the keys to success. I guess it's because I've also been so interested in making other people feel comfortable around me and because I take the time to care about other people. When it boils down to it, having good manners is simply about respecting and caring about other people. But in the long run, this perspicacity has been a big key to my success.

I've said this before. But isn't it worth repeating? Think about it. If you dress appropriately for each occasion; if you greet people warmly and correctly, shaking hands and looking them in the eyes; if you really listen to what they are saying; if you use proper dining etiquette when you eat out with them; if you are polite and honest and think about what's important to them; if you don't spend time texting and returning phone calls when you're with them (eating into their time with you); if you thank them appropriately and communicate logically, personably, professionally and thoughtfully in all your writing—whether it's email, social media or letters; then how can anyone not want to be around you, hire you, conduct business with you or respect you in return? At the very least, you'll have a better-than-average chance at success in all your endeavors.

It's true that today our youth is enamored with celebrity icons who don't reflect the best behavior. They watch the rude, selfish behavior of said "stars" and think they're cool. But in the long run, who really wins? Is it those who get in trouble, go to jail or develop "we-don't-want-to-work-with-you" reputations, or is it those who are ultimately admired and rewarded? Lindsey Lohan or Taylor Swift? Alec Baldwin or George Clooney? You get the picture. I'd say Swift and Clooney have the perspicacity for success. And, if you'll look closer at developing 21st-century manners and why they matter, you will too!

The Future of Children

How Can You Set Them up for Success?

How did Candidate B grow into a respectful adult? It started at home when he was a child. Every parent wants his or her child to be well-mannered and enjoyable to be around. However, many parents don't understand that they must model the behavior they want their child to follow. This includes language skills (no profanity, please!) and acting kindly toward friends, neighbors, relatives and pets—no matter how frustrating they might be. Most importantly, parents have to show their child the same respect they expect to receive from him or her.

But it goes beyond this. What about emphasizing the importance of family meal time? Enough of eating dinner in front of the TV, or everyone eating separately. So many families don't share meals together because numerous activities fill up their evenings. Incorporating time together in the evening is so important to developing good table manners and communications skills. Parents need to reinforce meal time and use it to talk about values as they relate to each family member's day! This should include teaching a child how to set the table and even cook meals for the family!

Parents can teach values by illustrating the importance of appreciating gifts that are given and kindnesses that are bestowed, such as by writing notes of appreciation. How many times have you seen a child receive a gift he or she didn't want? Instead of being sensitive to the giver, the child makes an unpleasant face and pushes the gift aside, making room for the next one. This shouldn't be tolerated but corrected when it happens. Parents should make an excuse to take the child to another room and quietly explain what is expected: smiling and thanking the gift giver for the present.

Parents should look for opportunities to show their child how to help others. Take your child to feed the homeless. Suggest that he or she volunteer for projects like picking up trash at school, in the neighborhood, etc. Encourage your child to help a classmate who needs a friend or help with a certain subject. It's a beautiful thing to see young people involved, excited and willing to take time out of their weekends to serve others. Young people just need to be reminded to look for these opportunities, and, once they find them, they suddenly stop focusing on their own needs and focus on the needs of others.

Finally, parents should teach their children to write thank you notes. Some ideas include: writing thank you notes to the mailman/mailwoman, the school janitor, cafeteria servers—anyone who doesn't usually get recognized for his or her hard work. Of course, thank you notes should always be sent after a child receives a gift or a kindness.

None of this is hard to incorporate into your life, and it will make a world of difference to the type of adult your child will become! An appreciative adult without a sense of entitlement but with a sense of compassion and good manners will stand out in any candidate lineup for the shrinking number of jobs in today's economy. You can make a difference in your child's future by showing him or her how to behave in the 21st century!

What Is Etiquette and Where Did It Originate?

People have asked me to write about the history of etiquette. So here it is. I was in the mood to find out more about who made up the rules in the first place!

It shouldn't surprise you that the French started it all! Today's etiquette began in the French royal courts in the 1600s and 1700s. Etiquette used to mean "keep off the grass." When Louis XIV's gardener at Versailles discovered that the aristocrats were trampling through his garden, he put up signs, or "etiquets," to warn them off, but the dukes and duchesses walked right past the signs. Finally, the king himself had to decree that no one was to go beyond the bounds of the etiquets. Gradually, the meaning of etiquette was expanded to include the ticket to court functions that listed the rules of where to stand and what to do. Like language, etiquette evolved, but in a sense it still means "keep off the grass." We watch for people to stay within certain bounds.

Before that, the first known etiquette book was written in 2400 B.C. by Ptahhotep. It reads as if it were prepared as advice for young Egyptian men climbing the social ladder of the day. One piece of advice was, "When sitting with one's superior, laugh when he laughs." Good manners have been around for a long time!

Even when people ate everything with their fingers, there were right and wrong ways to do it. Since ancient Rome, a lower class person has grabbed food with all five fingers while one of breeding has used only three, leaving the ring and little finger out of it. Thus, the raised pinkie as a sign of elitism was born. We do not, however, dare raise our pinkies today because this is a sign of pretentiousness and a sure indicator to the well-bred that one does not know the right way to eat, or worse yet, is a shameless social climber.

According to Esther B. Aresty's *The Best Behavior*, one of the earliest writers on civility was a "Friulian Italian," Tommasino di Cerclaria, known for his work *A Treatise on Courtesy*, c 1200. He did some moralizing but did so lightly and deftly. For di Cerclaria, carrying tales, betraying secrets and vainglorious boasting were faults that bordered on sin. Pushing ahead of others in a crowd was also evidence of poor breeding.

Around 1290, a Milanese monk, Bonvicino da Riva, wrote what is probably the first book dealing solely with table etiquette, *Fifty Courtesies of the Table*. Many of Bonvicino's rules were as elementary as those taught to little children today: do not loll at the table; do not gulp food and liquid in one mouthful; turn the head when coughing or sneezing; do not lick one's fingers clean of food or pick the teeth with the fingers; do not stare at others' plates; and do not talk with a mouthful of food. Some of the monk's rules were timeless and enduring.

American etiquette grew from these origins. Based on consideration for others, they still apply today.

Would you believe that the first actual record of American etiquette was George Washington's *Rules of Civility*? That's right, straight from the "father of our country." Later, in 1922, Emily Post published *Etiquette—*

In Society, In Business, In Politics, and At Home. Post, a self-proclaimed debutante-turned-writer/publisher, became a best-selling author and paved the way for others to preach good manners. She was followed by Amy Vanderbilt, who proclaimed herself "a journalist in the field of etiquette." Vanderbilt wrote *Amy Vanderbilt's Complete Guide to Etiquette.*

Letitia Baldrige and Judith "Miss Manners" Martin followed. Martin's newspaper columns resulted in her publishing several books, including *Miss Manners' Guide to Domestic Tranquility* in 1999.

Peggy Post, Emily's great-granddaughter, has followed in Granny's footsteps with *The Etiquette Advantage in Business: Personal Skills for Professional Success.* She also dispenses her rules of good behavior over the Internet.

Etiquette has expanded beyond society today. Many big businesses staff etiquette trainers to teach good manners to their executives. They teach everything from how to dress, how to act, how to eat and how to converse to writing good business letters. With globalization, executives are also being trained in respecting cultural differences to enhance their success rate in foreign markets.

With the number of etiquette books and coaches available, there's no excuse for not learning how to make other people feel comfortable and respected. But, you know the saying, "You can drag a horse to water, but you can't make him drink." In order for you to drink in good manners, you have to realize what's in it for you. If being successful in business, with people and in your life is part of your plan, then please start drinking in the information available to you to help you live your dreams.

What Is Respect?

On Veterans Day, my thoughts went to how much I respect the men and women who have served in the military, both past and present. This led me to muse about why I respect them so much. Is it their unselfishness? Maybe it's the fact that they stand up for an ideal for which they are willing to die?

It always amazes me at how respectful they are to others—their superiors, people on the street, people in war-torn countries who need their help.

Doesn't respecting others start with self-esteem? And doesn't self-esteem grow from self-confidence and knowing how to react in any situation? It's certainly a good basis.

Many of the students with whom I work haven't always had access to the best examples of how to respect others. The best way for them to learn is for them to understand that respect has to begin with the simple rule of treating others the way you would like to be treated. Making others comfortable when they are around you is a good start. How do you do that?

Here are some thoughts:

- Greet others with a smile.
- Firmly shake the hand of those you greet.

- Look people in the eye when you speak to them. When you don't, it makes them feel insecure.
- Listen to others rather than talking only about yourself.
- Say "please" when you ask for something.
- Say "thank you" when someone says something nice to you, gives you a gift or helps you in some way.
- Thank people after meeting with them.
- Say what you mean, and mean what you say—in other words, don't lie; tell the truth; be honest.
- Help other people whenever you can. Help those less fortunate. You'll be amazed at what a confidence-builder that is.
- Honor your parents, grandparents, children and relatives; honor your family and friends and those in positions of authority. Don't treat them with disrespect.
- Respect your elders; after all, they've lived longer and have had more experience than you.
- Love your country, your community and your environment. We all need to belong, and being part of something you love is the greatest bond.
- Open the door for others to enter first. Pull out a chair for your companion or elders at the dining table.
- Use proper table manners.
- Be kind to service staff. Look them in the eye and thank them.

- Don't be self-absorbed. Look outward, not inward.
- Don't bully or make fun of others. Defend those who are victimized by bullies.

It's pretty simple, really. Believe in yourself and others—honor them—just as our military men and women, both past and present, have honored this country.

Respect and Success – The 11 Traits of a Respectful Person

Let's face it. When you're young, you're always trying to figure out "what's in it for me" in every situation. For the most part, today's youth have gotten used to a feeling of entitlement. It all started back in the '80s when parents took the tack of having their kids "heard and not just seen," the opposite of what earlier generations expected.

No matter the cause, I've found that when working with teens, it clearly helps them get a grip when they understand why being respectful matters. Too often we assume they know these things when they actually don't. This was brought into sharp focus in one of yesterday's classes. In this case, actions spoke much louder than words. Kids were texting and talking among themselves on top of not watching me while I talked to them. One boy was sleeping. A couple were even rolling their eyes. This was the last straw.

"This class is about respect for people as much as it's about learning the basics of a good handshake." I was firm and direct. I came down on them without talking down to them. "How would you feel if you were in my place as the teacher and, with my body language, I let you know I couldn't care less about what you were saying?"

They all agreed that, as they put it, "It sucks the way we're acting."

I explained to them that I have a lot of respect for them and what they are going through during this time in their lives. "I'm only trying to help you and ask for the same respect back from all of you." I stressed how we can have conversations or disagreements with respect for each other without yelling or talking down, and that was what I was trying to illustrate to them at that moment. I smiled and announced, "Next time someone falls asleep in class, I'll ask him to excuse himself and go to the office to take a nap." It was important for them to know what I wouldn't tolerate.

Next, I challenged them with, "What do you think are the qualities of a respectful person?"

The comments were, "Respect your elders, be nice, blah, blah, blah."

My response: "Really? You think respect is only about being nice to your elders? Boy, have I got some details for you! Let's look at the traits of a respectful person and how having them will get *you* what you want in life."

Trait #1: They're honest. They don't lie. People can depend on them. Think of the heroes we admire in books, movies and real life. Don't they act with honesty and integrity? Aren't they generous with others? Doesn't everyone look up to them?

Trait #2: They don't lose their tempers, scream, yell or strike out against others when things don't go their way. In other words, they rarely lose control. When negative things happen to them, they remain positive. They treat people as they would like to be treated.

Trait #3: They are tenacious. They don't give up easily. They become resourceful when the going gets rough. They totally get that they can't change other people or the circumstances, but that they can change their attitudes about situations.

Trait #4: They admit when they're wrong. Instead of sticking to their guns (no matter what) just to be "right," they fess up to their mistakes, particularly when it lets another person "off the hook" or eases a situation.

Trait #5: They aren't lazy; they strive. They are hard workers who always want to "get it right."

Trait #6: They have their priorities straight. They put what is truly important, what will really help others or a situation, above their own needs.

Trait #7: They have an inner sense of right and wrong. They innately know the right thing to do, and they understand clearly when an injustice is being served.

Trait #8: They tend to be role models for other people. Others admire and look up to them.

Trait #9: They are givers. Most successful people are. They know the "secret" that the more you give, the more you receive when you are genuine about your gifts. We're talking not so much about money but time and expertise. They operate on Zig Ziglar's quote, "You will get all you want in life if you help enough people get what they want."

Trait #10: They have high self-esteem. They believe they deserve success and know they can do anything they go after. They know that a mistake is something they do and not who they are. They keep a positive self-image because they know that self-esteem is a state of mind that they have chosen.

Trait #11: They are loyal, even when it's tough to be. They stand behind those with whom they have forged relationships and don't betray them.

At this point, my students were all listening intently. I explained further. "If a person has all these traits, how will that help him be successful? Isn't it obvious? These are the qualities of highly successful people in our society—I'm talking Bill Gates, Oprah, Warren Buffet, George Washington, Abraham Lincoln and the like. It isn't a coincidence that both highly respected and highly successful people possess these traits."

The student who fell asleep raised his hand and asked, "So, by being a respectful person and having the traits you listed, success will find me?"

"Exactly," I replied. "Like an oncoming train!"

What Is Loyalty?

By definition, loyalty is faithfulness or devotion to a person, country, group or cause. It's one of the keys of business etiquette. Most employers share the concern that their employees may be disloyal. Disloyalty spans a wide spectrum from merely intentionally failing to perform tasks, to accepting personal benefits that rightfully belong to the employer, to dishonesty and theft. I once knew of an employee who routinely raided his employer's toilet paper, paper towel and coffee supplies for his own household use!

Disloyalty can also follow an employee who leaves an employer, taking with him as much business as he can along with what the employer considers proprietary and confidential information.

But it can go deeper. Promising to complete a task in an emergency and failing to do so. Taking advantage of the employer's good will and generous nature. Always looking at the job from the "me" perspective and not from the company's. And, particularly, when the employer needs his or her employees to morally support the company, and they fail to do so.

It's easy in today's economy to think about "me" rather than others, but here's the danger. Most other people will view those they see being disloyal negatively.

Word spreads quickly, and most marketplaces are smaller than you think. If you are disloyal, word has a way of spreading and ultimately damaging your work credibility. Why? It's all tied up with integrity, trust and that big, important concept called *RESPECT*. Being disloyal conveys a lack of integrity and respect and instills distrust in others.

People don't hire those who have a reputation for being disloyal and lacking integrity and respect for others, and they don't hire people they don't trust.

It works both ways. When a company does not reward loyalty or even acknowledge it, when employees are not respected and are taken advantage of and betrayed, that organization becomes one where potential employees don't want to work.

FIRST IMPRESSIONS

THE FIRST SEVEN SECONDS AND BEYOND

First Impressions – How to Create Lasting Business Relationships

I've written about first impressions before, but I like what Lydia Ramsey has to say and wanted to include it here. There's great advice here. Thanks, Lydia, for letting me share it:

Can you establish a lasting business relationship in just seven seconds? You can if you make a great first impression. Seven seconds is the average length of time you have to do it, and everyone knows that you won't get a second opportunity. A positive first impression can turn a chance encounter into a long-term association.

Whether that initial meeting is face-to-face, over the phone or online, you do not have time to waste. It pays for you to understand how people make their first judgment and what you can do to be in control of the results.

1. Learn What People Use to Form Their First Opinion When you meet someone face-to-face, 93 percent of how you are judged is based on nonverbal data—your appearance and body language. Only 7 percent is influenced by the words you speak. Whoever said that you can't judge a book by its cover failed to note that people do. When your initial encounter is over the phone, 70 percent of how you are perceived is based on your tone of

voice and 30 percent on your words. Clearly, it's not what you say—it's the way that you say it.

2.   Choose Your First 12 Words Carefully

Although research shows that your words make up a mere 7 percent of what people think of you in a one-on-one encounter, don't leave what you say to chance. Express some form of thanks when you meet a potential connection. Perhaps it is "Thank you for taking time to see me today" or "Thank you for joining me for lunch." People appreciate you when you appreciate them.

3.   Use the Other Person's Name Immediately

There is no sweeter sound than that of your own name. When you use a person's name in conversation within your first twelve words and the first seven seconds, you are sending a message that you value the other person. Nothing gets other people's attention as effectively as calling them by name and giving them your full attention.

4. Pay Attention to Your Grooming

Others will. In fact, they will notice your hair and face first. Putting off that much-needed haircut or color job may cost you a relationship. Very few people want to do business with someone who is unkempt or whose hairstyle does not look professional. Don't let a bad hair day cost you a connection.

5. Keep Your Shoes in Mint Condition

People will look from your face to your feet. If your shoes aren't well maintained, others will question whether you pay attention to detail. Shoes should be polished and appropriate for the business environment. They may be the last thing you put on before you walk out the door, but shoes are often the first thing other people see.

6. Walk Fast

Studies show that people who walk 10-20 percent faster than others are viewed as important and energetic—just the kind of people with whom others want to do business. Pick up the pace and walk with purpose if you want to impress. You never know who may be watching.

7. Fine Tune Your Handshake

The first move you should make when meeting someone is to put out your hand. There isn't a businessperson anywhere who can't tell you that a good business handshake is a firm one. Yet time and again people offer up a limp hand. You'll be assured of giving an impressive grip and getting off to a good start if you position your hand to make contact web-to-web with the other person's. Once you're connected, close your thumb over the back of the hand and give a slight squeeze. You'll have an impressive handshake and the beginning of a good business relationship.

8. Make Introductions with Style

It does matter whose name you say first and what words you use when making introductions in business. Because business etiquette is based on rank and hierarchy, you want to honor the senior or highest-ranking person by saying his name first. When the client is present, he is always the most important person. Say the client's name first and introduce other people to the client. The correct words to use are "I'd like to introduce . . ." or "I'd like to introduce to

you . . ." followed by the name of the other person.

9. Never Leave the Office Without Your Business Cards

Your business cards and how you handle them contribute to your total image. Have a good supply of them with you at all times since you never know when and where you will encounter a potential client. How unimpressive it is to ask for a person's card and hear the words, "Oh, I'm sorry. I think I just gave away my last one." You get the feeling that this person has either already met everyone he wants to know or maybe didn't come prepared to do business. Keep your cards in a card case or holder where they are protected from wear and tear. That way you will be able to find them without a lot of fumbling around, and they will always be in pristine condition.

10. Match Your Body Language to Your Verbal Message A smile or pleasant expression tells people that you are glad to be with them. Eye contact says you are paying attention. Leaning in toward the other person engages you in the conversation. Use as many signals as you can to look interested and interesting.

In the business environment, you plan your every move with clients. You arrange for the appointment, you prepare for the meeting, you rehearse for the presentation—but in spite of your best efforts, potential contacts pop up in the most unexpected places and at the most bizarre times. For this reason, leave nothing to chance. Every time you walk out of your office, be ready to make a powerful first impression.

About The Author
Lydia Ramsey is a business etiquette expert, professional speaker and corporate trainer as well as the author of Manners That Sell – Adding The Polish That Builds Profits. *She has been quoted or featured in* The *New York Times,* The Wall Street Journal, Investors' Business Daily, Entrepreneur, Inc., Cosmopolitan *and* Golf Digest. *To learn more about her products and services, visit her Web site www.mannersthatsell.com.*

How to Shake the Hand That Feeds You

Have you ever been introduced to a person and, when the traditional handshake took place, felt like you had just caught hold of a wiggly fish? There's nothing that is more of a turn-off than a wimpy handshake from someone in business!

The tradition of the handshake began in Egypt before the time of Christ. It originated as a gesture of peace, indicating that the hand held no weapon. One man would extend his right hand to show that he held no weapon and came in peace. The other would do the same, and then they would shake hands firmly. A firm grasp of the hand while the web of each person's thumb and forefinger touched indicated that each was powerful yet desired to be friends. This has become the preferred greeting worldwide.

The best way to greet a person is to stand and put your lead foot forward. (The lead foot is usually the one opposite from the hand with which you write.) Putting this foot forward puts you on very firm ground and makes you feel in control of yourself. Look the person directly in the eye and hold that eye contact until at least the end of the handshake. This is done to show the other person you can be trusted.

The first 7-20 seconds of a meeting among new people are the most critical to giving a good, confident impression. Starting off with a bad first impression can take a long time to overcome. In the case of an interview of any sort, you may not have the time to redeem yourself.

How to Create Your Image

Creating an image in the business world isn't as difficult as you think!

It's more than just getting up, dressing well and showing up on time. It's about managing an image once it's been created. Consistency is the key. Here are some suggestions that will help you get started.

Suggestion One

Start creating your image around your junior year of high school, if not before. How? Watch what you post on social media sites and on the Web. Why? Because what shows up on the Internet will stay with you forever. It's hard to conceive that anything posted during high school could potentially affect a career, but prospective employers and colleges are now using social media profiles as part of routine background checks. This means that scholarship organizations are likely doing the same, and their finding negative information could definitely impact your future. So, forget the provocative photos and the messages riddled with profanity. Be careful! You'll never know that those were the reasons you didn't get the job.

Suggestion Two
Smile. So many people don't smile; they frown instead! This is very off-putting. Develop a ready, genuine smile that will help you connect positively with others in any situation. Don't let social anxieties overwhelm you. Smiling can help you get through any situation. It's a secret weapon that totally disarms people and draws them to you.

Suggestion Three
Be a leader, not a follower. Create positive trends and habits that draw positive people to you. You can accomplish this through your stylish dress; encouraging and outgoing actions; and willingness to help others. Self-absorption will only produce a negative reaction in most people. Don't know how to be outgoing with others? Start by volunteering some time to help those less fortunate than you. You'll quickly learn that your life is fairly wonderful compared to others, and this will teach you how to reach out and encourage other people.

Suggestion Four
Marketing yourself later in life will be a lot easier if you have already made a statement at school or college with not only your family and friends but your community. Honoring and respecting others is the greatest tool you can have in your self-image toolbox. Part of honoring and respecting others is taking responsibility for not only your actions but also for part of your own livelihood as a teenager. Parents who teach their children how to be independent give them the greatest of gifts. Read about the early years of great leaders, and you will see how they were, more often than not, hard workers from an early age who learned how to think and act independently, and

who avoided depending on others for the "things" they wanted out of life. So don't sit around and wait for your parents to "give" you what you want—go out and earn it!

These aren't the only suggestions you should utilize to create a solid image for yourself, but they are the foundation for creating and managing everything else you do as you build a professional business image.

Image Breakers

Let's think about image breakers; you know, things like chewing gum during a business meeting, constantly interrupting people when they are speaking or crossing the familiarity line with coworkers.

I polled numerous etiquette coach friends to see what they thought. Here's a list of image breakers:

- Answering one's cell phone during a conversation or meeting
- Using profanity in public or online
- Gossiping, lying and blaming others for your mistakes
- Constantly disagreeing with people instead of showing respect, optimism and tact
- Using poor grammar and a limited vocabulary; mispronouncing words
- Asking a question and not paying attention to the response
- Not maintaining eye contact with the person with whom you are speaking
- Talking about yourself instead of listening to others
- Constantly sighing or rolling your eyes while someone is talking
- Giving a poor handshake

- Giving a woman too firm of a handshake
- Slouching
- Wearing too much makeup or skirts or pants that are too short
- Failing to dress appropriately for the circumstances
- Having bad breath or body odor
- Having an unpolished appearance, including dirty hair and nails; unkempt facial, ear and nose hair; general poor grooming
- Failing to check your clothing, hair, teeth and face before leaving the lavatory and arriving with clothing askew, hair untidy or something in your teeth or on your face
- Wearing badly polished shoes or rundown heels
- Having a stain on your tie, or elsewhere
- Having missing buttons or torn or frayed clothes
- Wearing clothing that is too tight, too low, too short or looks like it is about to wrestle with the contents
- Having inappropriate accessories (too many, too noisy, out of proportion for the wearer)
- Being age-inappropriate in clothing and accessories
- Wearing short socks just above the ankle instead of long socks to the knee (men)
- Not being aware that in some cultures, eye contact is considered rude
- Allowing self-importance to dominate
- Being an incessant "talker"
- Sitting first (men) at the dining table before women are seated
- A man following a woman while climbing stairs
- Getting drunk and talking loudly in public

• Staring at a woman's cleavage instead of her face
• Twirling your hair
• Biting your nails
• Drumming your fingers on the table
• Fidgeting in your chair
• Pacing while waiting
Quite a list.

Take the test. See if you are guilty of any of these image deal breakers. If you are, you know what to do. Just stop!

Body Language in Business (The Art of . . .)

Connecting to a person means making it clear how the content of a spoken message should be interpreted. Unfortunately, sometimes we are unable to deliver our messages by spoken or even written language, so we use body language to supplement what we want to say by gesturing, moving or making facial expressions.

Our body language sends a message to the other person, saying things like, "I'm bored and uninterested," or "I'm interested and excited to be here." No matter what words you use, your body language will always give you away. *The body doesn't lie!*

In order to be a successful body language communicator, keep the following in mind:

Sitting

Take care in the way you sit, for no other position connotes so much on its own. Think of the diversity of sitting positions that you've seen in business meetings, from practically horizontal to alert and upright. Sit upright. Never slouch. Sit with a straight back and with your legs together in front of you or crossed, either at the knee or at the ankle. Normally, women don't cross their legs, but men are allowed to. Avoid jiggling your knee, which is a sign of nervousness (and can be pretty annoying to people sitting near you). Keep your hands away from your face. Always face the person with whom you are speaking or to whom you are listening. If you don't, you'll come across as uninterested. Think of it as trying to impress someone you're interested in. Think about making yourself bigger and puffing out your chest.

Standing

When you stand, keep your back straight, with your midsection in alignment with your back (shoulders back and head up). This shows that you are comfortable with yourself and at ease in the situation. Slouching, sticking your belly out, stuffing your hands in your pockets and folding your arms defensively all suggest aggressive unease. When you slouch with your arms folded across your chest, you give the impression that you are tired, defensive and uninterested.

Hands

Some people talk with their hands; others stand with their hands glued to their sides. Most people haven't the foggiest notion what their hands are doing when they talk. Do you scratch your nose, your ears or your eyelids when speaking? All of these can be a sign of deception. Other movements to avoid include: pointing fingers, wringing your hands, knuckle cracking, picking your fingernails and playing with your pocket change. If you talk with your hands, you're going to come across as distracted or nervous. Keep your hands at your sides, or place them in your lap if you don't know what to do with them. Steepling the hands is a sign of high confidence.

Rubbing the chin or placing the hand under the chin with one or two fingers on the cheek is a sign of contemplation or evaluation.

Using your hands is effective sometimes, aggressive other times and irrelevant most of the time. Controlling your hands takes effort and willpower. Monitor your hand movements. Avoid making sweeping, cappuccino-clearing gestures during meetings. If you have to, sit on your hands!

Head Movements

Head movements communicate important information. Nodding in agreement can be immensely helpful to others, but too much nodding makes you look like a bobble-head doll! Shaking your head can signal disagreement or disapproval, but avoid shaking your head too much.

Eye Contact

Eye contact is critical to conveying that you are interested. Letting your gaze wander around the room illustrates disinterest. Looking at your lap or the floor shows that you are not self-confident and feel insecure. Looking someone directly in the eyes while speaking with him or her will assure the other person of your self-esteem, confidence and ability to get the job done. It will also relay a feeling of trust.

Smile

Nothing can make a person feel better than a smile from another. To brighten someone's day and show off your positive attitude, smile. A frown will always set the wrong tone.

"Tells" that will Aid you in Business

1. To spot a liar, look out for these four "tell-tale" signals. Non-verbal cues are unconscious giveaways of dishonesty. A specific cluster of non-verbal signals has been proven

statistically to be a highly accurate indicator of deception. These are:

- hand touching
- face touching
- crossed arms, and
- leaning away

According to research conducted at Northeatern University, if you see these "Tell-Tale Four" being displayed together, watch out!

2. To reach an agreement, send early engagement signals.
Carol Kinsey Gorman, in her *Forbes* article "10 Simple and Powerful Body Language Tips for 2013," noted: "Over the years, I've noticed that parties are more likely to reach an agreement if they begin a negotiation by displaying engaged body language (smiling, nodding, mirroring, open gestures, etc.) Interesting, that positive result is the same whether the display was the product of an unconscious reaction or a strategic decision."

3. To maximize your authority, curb your enthusiasm.
In the same article, Gorman also wrote, "If you are an extrovert, you most likely make a favorable first impression—because we are drawn to passionate people whose emotions are easily read. But when your communication style lacks of nuance and subtlety, your over-exuberance can overwhelm (or exhaust) an audience. So in situations where you want to maximize authority— minimize movements. Take a deep breath, bring your gestures down to waist level, and pause before making a key point. When you appear calm and contained, you look more powerful."

Fake it until You *Become* It

Want more in-depth information about what body language can do for you?

Watch this video with Amy Cuddy on body language (http://www.youtube.com/watch?v=Ks-_Mh1QhMc&feature=player_embedded). It's 21-minutes long but is *well* worth the watch. You'll be amazed at all you will learn.

TIPS FOR JOB INTERVIEW PREP

Interview Preparation – Communications Technology Part 1

What Needs to Happen Before an Interview?

Cell Phones

What does your voicemail message say about you? If I call you and get, "This is James, dude. Wad up? Give me a call," what kind of impression have you given me? Your message should reflect a professional tone with a concise message. Do you want your potential boss to be greeted with "Wad up"? So, just until you get a job (so your friends don't think you're a dork), change it. Once you have a job, consider using a less casual greeting for the sake of preserving your career!

I suggest something like, "Hi, this is James. I'm sorry I can't take your call right now, but if you leave me your name and telephone number I will get back to you as soon as possible. Thanks for calling."

In addition, I propose checking your ringtones to be sure they are standard. Once you begin interviewing, always set phones on silent or vibrate.

It's important to realize that the people you are with should always take precedent over phone calls or text messages. Some important business phone etiquette to remember:

- Let your voicemail take your calls while meeting with people.
- Return all phone calls within 24 hours.
- Do not make or receive calls during business meetings.
- If you are expecting an important call that cannot be postponed, alert the people in your meeting prior to the start of the situation; if and when you receive the call, step away from the meeting and keep the call brief.
- Always be courteous to people within hearing distance and use discretion when discussing private matters. Keep your voice low.
- When receiving a call in a restaurant, always step outside or to a place of privacy.
- Do not use your cell phone for talking or texting while driving unless you have a Bluetooth device.
- Never text while in motion.
- Text messaging while in a meeting should only be used in extreme circumstances and emergencies.
- Never text message during religious services, funerals, weddings, court proceedings or while sitting at a dining table.
- If you receive a text message about an urgent matter, remove yourself from your surroundings before answering.

When I go to meetings, my cell phone stays in the car. If I think I might need it to provide contact information during the meeting, it stays in my pocket on vibrate or turned off. I don't let anything disturb me *unless* it's critical. Then I keep it on vibrate and ask others to forgive me. "I might receive a critical call related to a current project and have to be available. Please understand."

I certainly understand when others are in that position. But when they're not, I'm so put off when people I'm at a meeting with start taking calls or messages during my time with them. Taking phone calls or texting others tells those you are with that they aren't as important to you as the person on the phone.

Be Aware of the Unspoken Messages You Send to People
How did this mindset come about for me? When my granddaughters were 13 and 14 years old, they used to visit my wife and me for two weeks every summer. At that time, I was extremely busy with work. I tried to be with them a lot, but I was always on my cell phone. During one visit, they drew a picture of my wife and me on the front of a thank you card they made for us. The picture showed my wife taking a tray of cookies out of the oven. I was standing next to her with a cell phone in my ear. The note was really sweet, and they never mentioned it, but when I saw that it hit me. I had been sending the wrong message to those kids!

From that summer forward, when I was with my grandchildren, my cell phone was off. I'd go out of the room and check messages away from them every few hours, but they never saw me with my phone stuck to my ear again. This was very powerful for me.

I share this story because I want you to understand the impression my grandchildren had of me. Sometimes we aren't aware of the negative impressions we create for others. When you are trying to spend quality time with friends and associates or trying to be attentive during a business meeting, remember what a friend of mine told me: "Just because your phone rings doesn't mean you have to answer it." When you are in a meeting or having dinner with someone, if you start texting, those who are physically present with you will feel that you don't care what they have to say.

Be aware of the unspoken messages you send to people.

Interview Preparation – Communications Technology Part 2

What Needs to Happen Before An Interview?

Email

Just as a cell phone voicemail message can give the wrong impression of you, an email address can do the same. Compare hotbody@hotmail.com to TomKnoley@TK.com. Which will impress a potential employer more?

While we're on the subject, let's discuss email etiquette. Most people are surprised that etiquette has anything to do with emails! But in business, email etiquette is essential. Keep these critical elements in mind when composing or responding to email.

- The subject line is there to inform the recipient of the purpose of the email. Keep it brief
- and relevant to the content.
- The content should be on the formal side. Always start with a salutation, such as "Dear Mr. King:"
- Always use a surname rather than a first name until advised that a first-name basis is acceptable. This may be advised purely by a return signature.
- Don't shout! Using ALL UPPERCASE LETTERS is considered CYBER SHOUTING!

- Remember: no email is private!
- Private matters should be discussed in person or on the phone.
- Always employ the 24-hour rule when sending an emotion-packed message. Cool down and be sure to reread your message before sending it.
- Always proofread all messages before sending them.
- Use a signature line containing your first and last name, company name and contact information at the end of every email. This is helpful for recipients who may need to contact you in other ways.

Social Networks

Before beginning your job search, take a look at your Facebook, MySpace and Twitter pages. Do you want your potential boss to know about your personal and social life? Should your prospective new employers see personal photos of you and your friends?

Check the content of your pages before beginning a job search and clean them up; delete anything you don't want your grandmother to read! That means photos and statements undesirable to potential employers. Be careful about voicing opinions regarding religious beliefs and political opinions, as well as music and hobbies. Stay conservative in content. Employers do check Facebook, Twitter and other social networks to see what you are like when you're not at work. Are you a wild party animal? Do you show off your tattoos and piercings?

One of my students displayed a photo of herself with a group of friends in bathing suits in a dog pile on the beach, all holding up Coronas. Even though they were close friends and the picture was totally innocent, I told her to clean it up.

"But it's on Facebook! It's private!" she said. She was indignant.

I explained that once something is on the Internet, forget it. It's not private. Look at Senator Weiner and Twitter, or Michael Phelps, the Olympic champion, smoking dope at a party in a YouTube video. Both of their reputations were damaged because of this. Everyone has to conduct themselves carefully, especially when they are trying to create a good impression.

Remember, when you are in "job search mode," your job is to create great first impressions! This means checking out and modifying all your communications vehicles: phone, email and social media!

<u>Weed Your Garden</u>

Many people like the looks of dandelions, clover and horseweed in their gardens. They feel it transforms a stiff, manicured look into a very free, casual garden that adds their personality to the space. Just as with gardens, others find that slashes of hot pink dye running through their hair adds to their personal style. Some with tattoos crawling up their arms and around their necks feel they are expressing that "This is who I am!" That may be, but pardon me while I overuse the old saying, "There's a time and a place for everything." An interview is not one of those places.

A friend of mine, who is in his early thirties and holds a college degree, called me the other day and was very upset that his year-long job search hadn't secured him a new position. He'd had wonderful interviews with some top corporations, sometimes even getting into the final selections. Then nothing! A short email usually followed with a "Dear John note" indicating that after careful consideration they had decided to hire another person. "What's going on?" he wondered. He asked me for my advice. We got together and did an analysis of how each of the interviews went from start to finish.

Once we began, I asked if he would share his Facebook page with me. OMG! That was it. My friend is quite the party animal in his off-hours and can get pretty graphic in his comments about other people, places and things. To put it mildly, there were a number of pictures on his page that his mother should never see, much less a potential employer! (Oh, you think potential employers don't check out your FB Page? Think again.) Additionally, his comments on different subjects surrounding politics were very blunt and didn't leave any room to speculate on where he stood in that arena. I told him that we had to do an overhaul on the page and change it up, getting rid of the pictures in question as well as a number of the comments. After his Facebook page, we moved on to his email account, getting him a new one with a different name (that dropped the nickname he often went by with his friends) to give it a professional air. The new account was set aside only for passing out to prospective employers. (johndoe@hotmail.com works a lot better than hotbody@hotmail.com!)

Next, we went on to his outgoing message on his cell phone voicemail. I hadn't realized until hearing it with different ears just how immature it sounded, so that got the axe as well.

I have known this guy for a number of years, and I can tell you he is good-looking and charming, as well as very smart. As wild as he can be, he is very serious and professional when it comes to work. BUT . . . from viewing and hearing his voicemail and Facebook, I would have a hard time believing it if I didn't know him so well.

The moral of the story: Weed your garden before you have the garden club over, especially if you want to have the featured spot on their Spring Tour!

Note: Am I starting to sound like a broken record? Good. I can't impress this stuff upon you enough!

Job Search Etiquette

I recently hired an assistant, but I still can't forget one particular interviewee. His interviewing skills were so atrocious that his actions struck me as almost comical.

When he entered my office 15 minutes late for the interview, he shuffled up to me in his unkempt, ill-fitting jeans and a long shirt, half tucked-in and half out. I don't think he was wearing a belt, because he kept pulling up his pants. His face sported stubble, and his hair looked unwashed. It was kind of like he just rolled out of bed and came to the interview! I extended my hand to shake his, but what I got was something like a fish hanging on the end of my hand. I shrugged it off, smiled and told him, "I'm so glad to meet you." He said nothing in reply. Instead, he did what can only be described as "plopping" into the chair near my desk.

At this point, I was wondering whether I was being punked because I'm a business etiquette coach!

His lack of interest was amazing. He never looked me in the eye but let his gaze wander around my office. Then, he whipped out his iPhone to check his messages. I was somewhat speechless but gathered myself together and asked him for his résumé.

"Oh, sorry, forgot it. Was in a hurry," was his eloquent reply.

So I asked him about his past experience. Now that's when he came to life. He sat up and began to dish on his former employer, heaping nothing but story after story of what a miserable dude the guy had been, what a lousy workplace (it seems they didn't have the right kind of coffee machine), and then he immediately asked me, "What does this gig pay?"

It was at that point that I told him that we wouldn't be a good fit and invited him to leave!

Which Interview Strategies to Adopt

What was I expecting, anyway? I expected him to be on time, dressed professionally in a clean and pressed pair of slacks, a nicely tucked-in and pressed shirt, a belt and clean shoes, along with well-groomed personal hygiene. (That means bathed, clean hair and nails and a shaven face.) A proper greeting would have been nice as well. He should have walked into my office with "Hello, I'm John Doe, and it's so nice to meet you." At that point, he should have extended his hand, grasped mine firmly and given me a solid handshake, while looking me directly in the eyes with a smile.

He should have waited for me to invite him to sit down, and he should not have sprawled into the chair but sat down with his legs bent at a 90 degree angle, not a straight line in front of him! He should have sat up straight and looked at me with interest, not letting his eyes wander everywhere but at me.

He should have brought copies of his résumé and any other pertinent material to give me a better idea of his past experience, and he should never have said one bad thing about his former employer. Better yet, he should have picked out specific areas or tasks that he enjoyed at his previous job to discuss and perhaps provided me samples of some of his work. *He should have done research on my company and prepared three important questions to ask me about it.* In other words, he should have shown me why he was perfect for the open position I was trying to fill.

Finally, if he had been smart, he would not have brought up the subject of money in the first interview. Actually, it's always best to let the employer bring up the topic of salary. By asking about salary upfront, the rude interviewee was showing that all he cared about was the pay and not the job itself.

How a Successful Candidate Handles the Interview and Follow-Up

The person I did hire had adopted all the right interviewing strategies. His appearance was impeccable. He answered all my questions in a straightforward, respectful manner, always looking into my eyes. He offered positive examples of his past work. He asked me intelligent, well-researched questions about my company. He left his references, along with samples of his work and another copy of his résumé. In addition, he followed up with me immediately with a handwritten thank you note and a phone call a week later. He did so professionally, and with a decent interval between contacts. Employers don't consider this pestering as long as the candidate is professional. I was glad that my new hire handled his contact with me so professionally. I'm a busy person, and I was impressed with his quiet but no-nonsense persistence.

How to Handle References

When I checked my new hire's references, it was obvious that he had done his homework with them. I had all the proper contact information, and they knew about the job position that he was seeking with me. I was really impressed on his first day in the office when he asked permission to call his references (on his own time) to let them know he got the job and to thank them for their help. Now, this is the caliber of person I want working for me!

Jump Start your Job Search

Here's an idea for you. The holiday season is the perfect time to **NETWORK**. It's a particularly good time for college students to start creating relationships before they actually need work and when they are just starting to look for a first job. What's the subtle way to do it? Go out to events, connect with professionals and ask their advice. Find out about their careers. People love to talk about themselves. Take advantage of that. In doing so, share a little about your own career goals . . . and watch your network grow! Having a network is one of the number 1 best tools you can have in your Job Search Kit!

Many job seekers don't realize how important it is to perform a search during these months. There is little to no competition. Companies are completing their budget planning for the next fiscal year, so it's a great time to get in front of hiring managers. And many executives have to fill openings early in the year or they may lose the budget for that position.

Create an image as a **SELF-STARTER**. Owners and managers of businesses view self-starters as key elements in a successful team. Why? Because they work hard to achieve their goals, and that's a big benefit to organizations.

Don't forget that **LOOKS COUNT**. Your appearance influences the bottom line on whether to hire you or not. While you can't change your physical being, you can show it off in the best possible way. This means being well-groomed (hair, face, teeth, nails) and wearing the appropriate clothing, shoes and accessories (clean, pressed, professional, polished, etc.). Don't expose tattoos, wear too much jewelry or overdo it. Just try to be as professional as possible.

When interviewing, **FOCUS ON HOW YOU CAN HELP THE COMPANY** become more successful. Avoid emphasizing what the company can do for you. How do you accomplish this? By outlining your strengths and pointing out the specific areas where you can help them solve their problems. Be ready to detail how you have stayed current with technology and industry changes and how the economy has affected the organization.

Older job hunters shouldn't be afraid to stress to prospective employers that they don't mind working for a younger boss—or to cite examples of times when they enabled a younger superior to succeed, grow and advance his or her own career. Emphasize that you will help your boss succeed in achieving his or her immediate goals so that he or she will have more time to work on what should be done in the future. Show that you are committed not only to your own success but to the success of the organization as well.

BE DIFFERENT. Show what separates you from the competition. Talk about the dramatically different things you do. Be prepared with some good stories that are exciting to talk about and illustrate your "difference."

Let the interviewer know that **YOU ARE A TEAM PLAYER**. Illustrate that you know the value of working with others and have a strong sense of being part of a team.

Present yourself as someone who is willing to give credit to others, is a good listener and is willing to take direction. If you are an older worker, let the interviewer know that you lead by example and want to mentor others.

DON'T ACT OVERCONFIDENT. Be conscious of what you say about your accomplishments and avoid coming off as a braggart or too much of a self-promoter. Be confident in what you bring to the table and express the results of your previous work, but don't be aggressively pushy about them.

Be prepared to **ANSWER THE TOUGH QUESTIONS**. Decide ahead of time how you will discuss the kind of reference you think your old boss will give you. This gives you a chance to talk about your previous position (if applicable) before the interviewer speaks to your former boss. However, a word of caution: don't use this as an opportunity to say anything derogatory about your former job! That's a definite mistake.

In this economy, **BE FLEXIBLE ON PAY**. In order to compete with others, especially younger job seekers, executives over 50 should be flexible with regard to compensation. Older employees have an advantage over younger job candidates if they are willing to accept a lower base salary in exchange for a larger performance-based bonus. Companies look for individuals who will take risks to prove that they are worthy of the job.

Don't try to be a jack-of-all-trades. **EMPHASIZE AN AREA OF EXPERTISE.** Previously, companies felt that employees who had skills in varied areas were desirable. When a company has to be understaffed, this makes sense. But if the organization is closer to being fully staffed, it will look for someone with a specific area of expertise, because this will have an immediate effect on the way the company does business.

MAKE SURE THE JOB IS RIGHT FOR YOU. If you are considering a job with a start-up, ask yourself several questions before accepting the position. Does the business have outside investors? How much of a burden will adding you have on the budget for that year? How will the company make money to support operations and generate profit?

Finally, **BE CAREFUL WITH YOUR ONLINE PRESENCE.** Make sure you don't have a controversial social media image. Don't have entries that are politically, religiously or sexually controversial or offensive. **FOCUS ON QUALITY SOCIAL MEDIA.** Make sure you engage quality followers and focus on how you interact with them and on your history of shaping discussions and the actions of your followers. It's not how many followers you have but what you do with them that counts. Organizations will differentiate among candidates who know how to engage people on social media. It's not how many followers on Twitter you have or that you are starting your own blog, but whether you have started following your potential employer's organization on Twitter or know what its blog is covering. Remember, **YOUR FACEBOOK PAGE CAN MAKE A FIRST AND LAST IMPRESSION ON POTENTIAL EMPLOYERS.** Unfortunately, social media has become an unavoidable character reference! What you post online tells your prospective employer how you will fit into the company environment and the job!

USE VIDEO ON LINKEDIN PAGES to show how you are different from others who do what you do! **UNDERSTAND THAT PEOPLE ARE PAYING ATTENTION TO YOUR EVERY SOCIAL MEDIA MOVE!** So, don't spend time playing games or participating in Facebook quizzes, because they give the impression that you are not very professional!

THE KEY IS TO ACT LIKE A PROFESSIONAL when you are searching for a new job! Happy hunting!

Job Hunting Tips – Fearless Job Hunting

Pegotty Cooper, a leadership and career strategy coach, says that two-thirds of white-collar jobs are found through conversations. In fact, a Standout Jobs and PBP Media Recruiting Trends Survey conducted in 2009 found that employers will spend less money on job boards and rely more on referrals. That's good news, right?

Well, the problem is that many job seekers won't reach out to their contacts for help, even though they know that this is the best way to find their next job!

Why? The answer goes back to *fear.*

What can be done to get rid of the fear of having new conversations and exploring what's out there to discover unexpected opportunities?

Cooper, in an article for the American Society of Association Executives, proposes a six-step process to overcoming that fear:

1. Acknowledge the fear and just push on through it, recognizing that fear is normal and usually found between you and the things you most want.
2. Create your own story about who you are as a sought-after contributor to the workplace, and put a stake in the ground about what you are excited

about and eager to share in your own exploration of adding value to an organization.

3. Get comfortable in not having the next step thoroughly defined and nailed down. This is a time for exploration, and the person you are calling may have a key to the treasure. This could be an insight about how the industry or an organization works, some resources that would be valuable to you or another contact that may lead to the pot of gold.

4. Prepare a brief script as a security blanket so that you can refer to it if you have a brain freeze. This should include the question of whether this is a good time for a 10- to 15-minute conversation. Tell them why you are calling them and who referred you, state your intention for the conversation and make your request clear and simple so that they can say yes without concern for their time or reputation.

5. Schedule time in your calendar for making these calls, and list the calls by name with the phone number and referral source. Keep track of each phone call you make so that you can follow up with a thank you and any updates about how you used the information/contacts they provided.

6. Make it a game to expand your connections, and enjoy the adventure of exploring new territory. Track your results and celebrate your victories each day.

Good advice.

Think of all this as a *performance.* My friend Jeff Nelsen, professor of music at the prestigious Indiana University Jacobs School of Music and teacher of Fearless

Performance, says, "Fearless Performance is not necessarily the lack of fear, but rather the choice that there are things more important than fear." He's right.

Pegotty Cooper is a leadership and career strategy coach who works exclusively with association executives to uncover their greatest leadership strengths and to have them be authentic in their leadership skin. Visit her Web site at http://careerstrategyroadmap.com/.

*Follow Jeff Nelsen on Facebook via
https://www.facebook.com/FearlessPerformance?fref=ts
and https://www.facebook.com/jeffnelsen?ref=ts&fref=ts.*

Job Interview Techniques

Be on Top of Your Game

Having just celebrated the Easter holidays as I write this, I always think of Easter as a time of new beginnings and fresh starts. Life for the past few years has been very tumultuous and forced many into new beginnings. The unemployment figures have skyrocketed over the past few years but thankfully are starting to go in the right direction. The economy is slowly getting better in North America, and jobs are a little more available. However, the number of applicants out there is still very high comparatively. Why is this important for job seekers? Because it's more important than ever to brush up on job interview techniques and be on top of your game.

The game of landing a job has changed in many ways from what it was only five years ago. Oddly enough, companies are now looking more for the old values and actions than they were a few years ago. These practices that were once abandoned are now back at the forefront.

I have often written about the importance of the first 20 seconds of meeting someone, which can be a good or a bad thing depending upon what you make of it.

Appearance

The trendy shirt worn over the waistband has been changed to the well-dressed, put-together look that was in style years ago. Companies are looking for individuals who know how to put themselves together with style and grace. Why? The casual workplace has been replaced with a much stiffer atmosphere that is more businesslike due to the fact that doing business today is much more difficult that it was five years ago. This means that companies and their employees must stand out in very positive ways to win business. It is a proven fact that a company is only as good as its team members, so the pressure on employees to come across in a professional manner has increased. Slacks and a plain-colored shirt convey that message more than a patterned shirt worn outside of nice blue denim jeans. Wall Street was dressing on the whole with a much more casual flair but has gone back to the suit and tie for men and dress suits for women, conveying the message that it is time to get down to business and look the part. Productivity is going up, and the economy will start to turn around with it.

The New Old Rules

At the very least, it's important to review old etiquette books to get a feel for the right tone and approach to handling interviews. This means researching how the interviewing company dresses, understanding its mission statement and preparing intelligent questions about the employer and the position for which you are interviewing. It means being focused on the interviewer, being well-mannered and following up with a written thank you note! All things I've been preaching for some time now! The basic rules haven't really changed, but in a lot of instances, people have decided to ignore them. Bad move.

Interviewing over a Meal

The power breakfast is gone for the most part, but lunches sans alcohol are back. This is a great time to have quiet conversation and to let the best you shine forward, but remember that a business meal is never about eating—it is about making the right impression. Be conscious of how you treat the waiter and eat with the correct utensils. It's not about how you eat nearly as much as it's about how you carry yourself. NEVER use your cell phone or respond to texts or calls during this time. Turn it off and leave it in a pocket or purse. Always prepare at least two questions to ask the interviewer at the end. Never say anything bad about former bosses or companies. Remember, attitude is EVERYTHING.

The jobs are out there now, but the competition is far more intense. Bone up on proper job interview techniques to place yourself in the best possible light.

<u>What to Wear to an Interview</u>
Interviewing for Teens

I'm going to share a typical class on "What to Wear to an Interview." Here's the scenario: We go to Macy's at the Paseo Nuevo Mall in Santa Barbara. Most of the guys show up in baggy pants or shorts and shirts. I tell them this style makes them look very young. My point is that they should impress upon potential employers that they have some knowledge behind them. Dressing well tells an employer, "I'm a good risk to hire." Wearing a style epitomized by gang members doesn't give the impression of someone they'd like to employ!

As usual, I discover that most of the boys don't know their waist sizes because they buy pants two to four sizes too large. I tease them, and they think it's funny. I have each of them take a pair of pants and button the waist and wrap it around their necks. The ends should just touch and the distance around will be equal to each guy's waist size.

I caution them to tuck in their shirts. "Why?" they question. I explain that tucking it in makes them look more put together. I show them how a man should tuck in his shirt so that it stays in and looks tidy.

"Drop your pants, pull your shirt down and flat across your belly and butt. Before you pull up your pants, put your hands in the pockets and make them flat. Then pull up the pants. If wearing boxers, go inside the pant and pull the boxers down. If you tuck your shirt in after the pants are buttoned, your shirt won't stay in and look neat."

I tell the guys not to wear two or three tee shirts under their regular shirt as they sometimes do.

I've learned from the girls that they think overdressing makes them look important. They want to use lots of jewelry and fill all their pierced ear holes. I explain that "less is more." I advise them to put out all their clothes the night before to make sure this is how they want to look. "Make sure everything is neat and pressed." Once that's done, and they are dressed, I tell them to remove one piece of jewelry. "You'll come off more conservative rather than flashy if you do."

Some of them complain. "But, I'm an artist and want people to see my personality."
I smile and say, "Save it until you've got the job. You want to make other people comfortable when speaking to you."

Why Do We Have to Dress Up?!
One boy complains, "I still don't see why we have to dress up."

I tell them my story about my first big client:

"I was going to make a very large presentation to Delta Airlines that I hoped would win me long-term business with the company. I wore a suit and tie (not my normal attire), because I knew that they did so. I did it to make them feel comfortable with me. As I got into my presentation, I began waving my hands and describing the event, and they were all smiling. I stopped and asked if I could take off my coat. They said yes and took off theirs as well. I went on to tell them how during the event a large jet would appear and blow people away. My enthusiasm increased and drew them into my story, taking them away with me. I got the job and spent the next decade producing events for them. But I initially made them comfortable with me by dressing as they did so that I could later let my personality win them over."

I also explained that overdressing and underdressing both send strong messages. Being underdressed says you are not interested in the interview. Overdressing is a better option than underdressing for the interview process. However, I encouraged them to practice the K.I.S.S. method—Keep It Simple, Silly!

I tell everyone to cover their tattoos and piercings if they can. Never wear anything religious, such as a cross or Jewish star. I explain that it's too emotionally charged in these times. I suggest that if they must wear such symbols to hide them under their clothing. I also advise them to remove all the jewelry from their piercings.

One girl cries out, "I can't take them off; they're still healing!"

I tell her to wait to interview until she can.

The Basics

So then we begin to talk about what to wear. I tell them that first and foremost, they should make sure they have:

- A neat appearance
- Clean hands and fingernails
- Brushed teeth
- Clean and combed hair
- A fresh smell
- Nice clothing

- Shined shoes

We talk about cologne and deodorant. I explain that it's important not to wear cologne. Why? People with allergies will go nuts with it. Who's to say the hiring manager won't be allergic? Overpowering cologne can be offensive. In addition, the sense that most triggers memory is smell. That's right. Smell can trigger both good and bad memories. For example, my mother always wore Taboo cologne. She's been gone now for 19 years, but every time I pass a woman who is wearing it, my mind immediately goes to my mother! And those memories are so warm and happy, but what if they hadn't been? What if she had been abusive? What if that happens with a hiring manager? It might mean you won't get hired.

It's also imperative that everyone wears deodorant to a job interview. I tell them that even if you don't normally perspire, when you get nervous, you will, and chances are you'll be nervous at a job interview. When you're nervous, your body gives off an odor. Deodorant is your defense mechanism.

Next I tell them to dress to impress. Dressing to impress isn't about how expensive the clothing is, but how you put it all together. It's about showing how *well put together you are.*

Tips
- If you find yourself in a hard financial situation, buy accessories that will make old outfits look new, such as ties, belts, vests, bracelets, earrings and scarves.
- I repeat—go for a conservative look, not a flashy one.
- Be comfortable, but present the BEST you that you possibly can.

What Not to Wear
For guys, I advise avoiding:
- Shirts with inappropriate messages
- Clothing that is too tight
- Cutoff jeans or pants
- Shorts
- Clothing that is too baggy
- Flip-flops
- Cologne
- Visible tattoos and piercings

For girls, I warn not to wear:
- See-through, low-cut or strapless blouses or dresses
- Heels that are too hard to walk in
- Clothing that is too tight
- Shoes that make a slapping noise when walking on wood floors
- Flip-flops
- Cologne or perfume
- Visible tattoos and piercings

I tell everyone to wear:
- Deodorant
- A conservative hair style—no unnatural colors

How Do I Put Together an Outfit?
Macy's stylist takes the students through all the choices of selecting an outfit for an interview.

For guys:
- A button-down shirt is a must-have in a male's wardrobe. It goes well with the tailored straight pant

or dark straight jean. But for a more professional look, the key is to tuck in the shirt.

- A crewneck tee under a shirt can substitute for a tie. It adds additional color to the outfit without the trouble of tying a tie. But make sure the crewneck tee is a basic color, like white, black or gray. Too much color is distracting.
- The tailored straight pant is another essential in a male's wardrobe. You can pair it with the button-down shirt or a nice V-neck sweater.
- The V-neck sweater is a great add-on to a professional outfit. You can pair it with either a button-down shirt or a basic crewneck tee.
- Again, jeans are tricky when matching tops to wear to an interview. The key is to look for dark jeans without any distressing or holes. Make sure they are straight— not too baggy and not too skinny, just perfect.
- Once you have the perfect professional outfit, add a clean-cut jacket to complete your interview outfit. Keep it simple and basic.

For girls:
- A classic white button-down blouse is a great basic. It goes well with any pant and jean. Pairing the classic white button-down gives an outfit a new touch and provides you with two outfits if you have a second interview.
- The perfect trouser is a must-have and works great for any interview. You can pair it with the classic white button-down (always tuck it in for a professional look) by itself or add a cardigan for another classic look.
- A basic blazer is another great essential to have in your professional wardrobe. You can pair it with the perfect

trouser or long and lean jeans for a casual business look.

- Pairing the blazer with a ruffled tee adds great texture to the outfit. Again, you can match it with the trouser or jeans mentioned above.
- Look for a jean with a more tailored look. Long, lean jeans are great for an interview outfit. Look for something with a slim fit and wide flare to give it more of a trouser look.
- The tank dress is great for an interview, but it should be paired with a cardigan. Make sure it isn't too short. The key with length is not to have the dress hang shorter than two inches from the knee.

I tell them to do the private school uniform test while deciding on a dress.

"What's that?" one of the girls questions.

I demonstrate. "Place your hands at your sides and make sure your skirt isn't shorter than where your fingertips end."

The parting thought? "Above all else, the key is to be clean, neat and fresh!"

Interview Tips for Older Candidates

Being 50+ and out of work is stressful. Often, that stress sends the wrong message in interview situations. The best way to handle anxiety and present oneself well is to be prepared! Here are some great tips from business and etiquette coaches and HR specialists.

- Look your professional best.
- Don't forget that with 50 years comes a wealth of experience.
- Smile and remember that your potential employer will feel more comfortable having you represent his company if he feels at ease in your presence.
- Don't try too hard. Fifty is the new thirty!
- Be prepared to work with people younger than you, so be flexible and have a youthful mind while carrying the elegance of a 50-year-old. Emphasize your ability to work with generational differences.
- Be positive and real, not desperate. Your experience and carriage should speak for you. Understand that employers value older workers because of their experience and ability to work within a team as well as their understanding, knowledge and practice of business etiquette and observance of company policies.

- Prepare three questions to ask about the company or job that are well-researched and will serve to impress the interviewer with your preparedness and interest.
- Be optimistic. Positive thinking is imperative. A "this next job is mine" attitude is essential.
- If you've been out of work for some time, don't focus on it with the interviewer.
- Refer to your résumé; don't treat it as a disconnected document, but tie it in to the interview.
- Don't give up or be dismayed if the process of interviewing for jobs takes longer than expected.
- Young or "old," first impressions are crucial. Be the best you can be.

What HR Specialists Say
- Research new jargon and the prospective company.
- Focus on your experience, not your years.
- Determine the hard-to-answer questions and how you will respond ahead of time. Example: When asked, "Aren't you over-qualified?" respond, "I'm uniquely qualified."
- Assure the prospective employer that you are in tune with the latest computer and technical skills (and be sure you are up-to-date).
- Be prepared to answer questions about specific situations in your previous jobs.
- Never air the dirty laundry from past jobs.
- Never bring up money. If the interviewer does, ask what he is looking for. Research salary levels so

that you have an idea of the going rate for the specific job.

- Don't show up early; you'll look too eager. Show up on time or just five minutes prior to the interview.
- Always write a handwritten thank you note. Wait a week, and follow up with a phone call to ask when you might expect to hear back.

Links to More Great Advice

http://www.kiplinger.com/columns/onthejob/archive/six-tips-for-job-seekers-over-fifty.html

http://www.careerbuilder.com/Article/CB-677-job-Search-Tips-for-the-Over-50-Job-Seeker/

<u>Things Not to Do in an Interview</u>

Lizandra Vega, recruitment, career and image expert, as well as author and blogger, shared some insightful information with me recently. She was kind enough to let me share it with you. Heed her words carefully:

You've spent weeks researching potential hiring companies, fine-tuning your résumé, and mentally preparing yourself for the interview challenge. Suddenly, an email arrives from a human resources director—not a manager—a director inviting you to interview for just the type of position for which you've been looking. You're so there, and your mind is saying, "This job is *mine!*" After all, you've got the experience, the credentials, the degree(s), plus extra certifications to boot. The interview day is here, and you are pumped. Yet, inexplicably, your chances of landing the job are quickly deflated before you even set foot inside the interview room. Were you mistaken for a similar candidate? Has the job been put on hold? Why does the recruiter seem so lukewarm on you before you've even had a chance to "strut" your stuff?

Commonly, recruiters and hiring managers become privy to clues you inadvertently display during the pre-interview stage—raising suspicion as to the type of employee you would be (if you were hired). When such "questionable" behavior is exhibited, there is little (if any) chance of turning it around. So before you go on your next job interview, prevent yourself from making one or more of these ten blunders, which quite possibly can end your interview before it begins.

1. **Risqué social media profiles/photos**: The first thing corporate and executive recruiters do these days after they've identified a viable candidate online is to look at their social media profile. Sometimes recruiters will wait to take a quick peek at your social media profile/photo right before they greet you in the reception area (so that it's fresh in their mind). A client took a pass on a "stellar" candidate who had recently added on Facebook that she "loved smoking pot." The candidate had also uploaded a new profile photo of her weekend partying while snuggling suggestively against a bottle of Bud Light. We were lucky not to lose the client, but the candidate lost the job opportunity.

2. **Inappropriate dress**: Job seekers will often underdress, overdress, or partially-dress for the interview, and those are definite reasons why they don't land the job. Underdressing in skimpy outfits, overdressing in sequined "Saturday date-night wear," or partially dressing and finishing up in the reception area (change your shoes outside) are sure indicators of your poor judgment. Even if you're interviewing within a creative environment or in 90-degree weather, flaunting your cleavage, shoulders, bare legs and toes may be more than the recruiter wants to see, and he or she certainly doesn't need you as the office trendsetter.

3. **Rude to the receptionist**: If you are rude to my receptionist, I know you will be rude to me, my clients, fellow employees, etc. Rude is rude! There is no combating such impoliteness. You may want to unload your frustrations on the receptionist, but front desk

receptionists are the eyes and ears of a company. News travels fast in an interoffice email from the receptionist to the human resources director, alerting him or her that the candidate he or she is about to see is ill-mannered and brash. So be particularly respectful and gracious to receptionists—they have more input on your candidacy than you think.

4. **Neglecting to bring a résumé**: If I hear one more job candidate use the "I want to save trees" excuse for not bringing a résumé with them, I'm going to lose it. Of all the lame excuses for not being diligent enough to supply a recruiter with a résumé, this is the one that most gets my blood boiling. You want to save a tree, so you put me through the trouble of printing a copy of your résumé (making me endanger a tree)? It comes across as neglectful and/or forgetful—qualities not highly regarded in the workplace. Let me make this perfectly clear. Even if you have emailed your résumé electronically, refrain from making the assumption that the recruiter will have it handy to refer to during your live interview. It is recommended that you bring between five and ten copies of your résumé to every interview.

5. **Refusing to fill out an application**: Nothing screams "BAD ATTITUDE" as much as refusing to fill out a job application or questionnaire. When you write "See Résumé" instead of filling out the information that is being asked of you, you are basically saying that you dislike complying with rules, that you like to make your own or that you're just plain lazy. Personally, that is the "writing on the wall" for future arrogant behavior.

6. **Punctuality (arriving either more than 15 minutes early or late)**: You may think that arriving to a job interview 30 minutes early earns you brownie points, but this is not the case. If you arrive more than 15 minutes earlier than your

scheduled time, you may be perceived as overly aggressive or desperate, or as someone who is not in high demand. If you are traveling from far away and you do arrive extra early (and want to use the restroom and fix yourself up), ask the receptionist not to announce your early arrival. Still, that doesn't guarantee that he or she will follow your instructions, and your premature arrival might be announced anyway. If you are going to be more than five minutes late, you must call. Expect a rescheduled interview or waiting for the recruiter's next time slot.

7. **Accepting/initiating cell phone conversations in the reception area**: Keep your babysitting issues, boyfriend troubles and other interview appointments under wraps. If you must make a phone call or accept an urgent call, excuse yourself from the reception area. Make a point of being discreet. You are being watched and listened to before your official interview begins. In fact, your official interview starts when you enter the office building's lobby and elevators (especially when there are cameras that can be played back).

8. **Rescheduling an interview more than once**: Emergencies do happen, but typically not more than once during one interviewing cycle. If something pressing in your life comes up and you must reschedule an interview, make sure you wait until the situation has cleared before you put it back on the calendar (even if it means losing out on that particular opportunity). The recruiter will appreciate your respect for his or her busy work schedule. Deferring an interview appointment more than once makes you seem unreliable and flippant about your interest in the company and the position.

9. **Social awkwardness**: Big "WARNING" signs go up for being socially awkward. Some of the most common social awkwardness faux pas I'm warned about by my

receptionist ("on the DL") are: nervous laughter, fidgeting, close-talking, self-talking and self-touching. Refusing to hang up your overcoat, unloading a wet umbrella or saying no to a glass of water may also come across as ungracious and awkward. My recommendation on the glass of water is to always say yes, even if you're not thirsty. This makes you seem amenable to a kind gesture, and water is both cooling and relaxing for your nerves. A side note to this suggestion: avoid popping meds with your water.

10. **Bringing a buddy along for support**: This is such a no-no! You wouldn't believe how many people go on interviews with a roommate, parent, husband, baby, out-of-town guest or parole officer (that one I sort of understood), and it is absolutely an interview killer. If you don't have the sense or confidence to go on a job interview without a sidekick, then maybe you're not ready for a lot of other challenges the work environment will present. You want to come across as an independent individual rather than one who relies on codependency. Coming with your baby in a carriage says you do not have the right childcare system in place and that you may therefore come to work with your child on a regular basis (unproductive for an employer).

Avoid shooting yourself in the foot before you even get that foot in the interview room. Carefully assess your pre-interview actions and behavioral choices—factors that weigh in to your candidacy as much as (or more so) your professional qualifications, education, recommendations and affiliations.

About the Author

To learn more about Lizandra Vega, go to http://www.lizandravega.com/about. Visit her Facebook page via

*http://www.facebook.com/LizandraVega.TheImageOfSuccess
and her Amazon Book Page at
http://www.amazon.com/Image-Success-Make-Great-
Impression/dp/B005CDUQDG/ref=sr_1_1?s=books&ie=UTF8
&qid=1357952029&sr=1-
1&keywords=the+image+of+success.*

<u>Interview Questions – Are There Only Three?</u>

George Bradt, a contributor at *Forbes*, wrote an article last year that combined the thoughts of top executive recruiters at a business leadership forum. In the article, he reports that the only three true job interview questions are:

1. Can you do the job? (What are your strengths?)
2. Will you love the job? (What is your motivation?)
3. Can we tolerate working with you? (Do you fit into the organization?)

That's it. Those three. Think back to every question you've ever posed to others or had asked of you in a job interview. Everything is a subset of a deeper in-depth follow-up to one of these three key questions. Each question may be asked using different words, but every question, however it is phrased, is just a variation of one of these topics: strengths, motivation and fit.

If you're the one doing the interviewing, get clear on what strength, motivational and fit insights you're looking for before you go into your interviews.

If you're the one being interviewed, prepare by thinking through examples that illustrate your strengths, what motivates you about the organization and role for which you're interviewing and the fit between your own preferences and the organization's Behaviors, Relationships, Attitudes, Values and Environment (BRAVE). But remember that interviews are exercises in solution selling. They are not about you.

Think of the interview process as a chance for you to demonstrate your ability to solve the organization and interviewer's problem. This is why you need to highlight strengths in the areas most important to the interviewers, talk about how you would be motivated by the role's challenges and discuss why you would be a BRAVE fit with the organization's culture.

Common Job Interview Mistakes

A new survey of over 2,000 hiring managers revealed the **10 most common mistakes job candidates make during a job interview**. Here they are, unveiled in David Letterman style:

10 Over-explaining why you lost your last job

9 Conveying that you are not over it

8 Lacking humor, warmth or personality

7 Not showing enough interest or enthusiasm

6 Inadequate research about a potential employer—lack of preparation

5 Concentrating too much on what you want rather than what you can do for the company

4 Trying to be all things to all people

3 "Winging" the interview

2 Failing to set yourself apart from other candidates

1 Failing to ask for the job!

The Finer Details

The little things really do matter. You need to make the interviewer's day! Why? Because he or she will want to nurture that relationship and hire you. One hiring manager assured us that if a job candidate makes her feel good about herself, then she knows that the candidate will make her clients feel good about themselves as well. That's what it's all about. This is how a job candidate can make himself stand out from the pack.

While I've listed the 10 most common interview mistakes, the finer details are well worth reviewing. So, here are 25 more!

- Failing to confirm the day/time/place of the interview
- Being late and failing to call ahead
- Failing to state your name clearly, not repeating the name of the interviewer to ensure that it is being pronounced correctly or not using the interviewer's name frequently throughout the interview (people love to hear their names, and there is a huge positive psychological effect when they hear it from the candidate
- Failing to acknowledge and respect the support staff, including security, the receptionist, the secretary or others encountered on your way in. The interviewer may ask their impressions of you
- Not bringing the necessary documents—several copies of your résumé, portfolio and completed application (if required)
- Not standing up to greet the interviewer or anyone else who enters the room during the interview— this is a sign of respect
- A poor handshake with no eye contact
- Failing to turn off cell phones, smartphones and any devices that might interrupt the interview with rings, dings, beeps, chimes, vibrations or other noise, and even, worse, using one's personal device during the interview

- A lack of focus and eye contact; being distracted
- Not dressing appropriately or showing good personal hygiene along with poor attention to detail; e.g., unpolished shoes; threads hanging from clothing
- Forgetting to smile
- Poor enunciation and too many "um"s
- Being uncomfortable or uneasy and not being "in the moment" to connect or inspire—little or no cultivation of a strong personal presence
- Having no awareness of the environment and its people
- Not knowing how you will respond to specific questions
- Not having three questions prepared about the company
- Being negative or dishonest
- Interrupting the interviewer but not showing good grace if you are interrupted
- Providing too much unnecessary information— over-answering the question, prattling on and on or not really listening to the question and thinking about the response
- Just blurting out something as soon as the interviewer stops talking because you're nervous
- Pretending to understand something you do not
- Lacking a personal online presence
- Wearing sunglasses during the interview
- Not using caution when posing questions about advancement and compensation; save questions about vacations, sick days, etc., for the HR representative
- Failing to thank the interviewer in person at the end of the interview session

And, of course, after the interview, always, always prepare and send a handwritten thank you note. Take advantage of sending the note to make a statement about what you feel you can do for the company and how much you would love to work for it!

What to Do after an Interview

The interview went extremely well. You had all the right answers ready to the questions asked of you. You'd done your research and threw in information during the conversation to let the interviewer know that you had read up on his company. He even commented on your well-groomed appearance and how he wished all people knew how to dress professionally like you. But now that it's over, what's next?

That's easy. First, write a thank you note to the person who took the time to interview you. Write it the same day as the interview. A thank you note is always better than anything else, because it is not done as often and will always stand out to potential employers. What should you include? Thank the person for his or her time. Include a sentence that describes how you will meet the company's expectations. The interviewer told you exactly what the company is looking for in a candidate. "Parrot" what you heard about the job in your own words and ask participating questions, such as "When shall I contact you?" Here's a sample.

Sample Thank You Note for Interview

123 Main Street || Central City, CA 91234 || 213-629-1234 || JohnDoe@GMAIL.COM
Date
Salutation Name
Title
Company
Address 1
Address 2
Dear (Salutation Name):
It was a pleasure meeting with you on (DATE). I would like to take this opportunity to thank you for taking the time to meet with me, as well as to express my appreciation for the information you offered. I am still very interested in the customer service position, and I am convinced, now more than ever, that it is the right job for me. I feel my background working in retail sales and the courses I have taken at Santa Barbara City College in customer service have prepared me well for just the sort of challenges and responsibilities we discussed.

I am eager to meet with you again to discuss my background and qualifications at greater length and how I can be of value to (COMPANY NAME). I understand that you will be making your decision in the next two weeks. Please feel free to contact me at the above number, or let me know when you would like me to contact you, so we can continue the discussion over the telephone that we began today.
Sincerely,

John Doe

Thank You Note Via Email
Write an email as a last resort. Why? People often misinterpret email message intent incorrectly.

The Waiting Game
After an interview, you are entitled to hear something back from the employer within a reasonable amount of time. Unfortunately, that doesn't mean you will. Ideally, you would have ended the interview by asking the employer what his timeline was for being in touch with the next steps. If you did and that time passes, then you have the perfect excuse to politely follow up. This time you can drop the employer a quick email, explain that you're still very interested but understand that hiring can take time and ask if he or she has an updated timeline.

If the company didn't give you a sense of the timeline in which a decision would be made at the end of the interview, you can follow up within a week or two of your meeting to reinforce your interest and politely inquire as to what the expected timeline for a decision might be. Don't just ask for an update—that's too easy to ignore, particularly if the employer doesn't have an update yet. Instead ask for a specific timeline.

Phone Manners Matter
When the call does come through:
• Be professional.
• Speak into the phone.
• Avoid background noise.
• Stay focused on the call.
• Be prepared to take notes.
• If you place the call, practice before initiating the contact.

Remember, when you're on the phone with a potential employer, stress why you are the perfect candidate for the job! Good luck!

Table Manners

Terri Fowler, a former food server, got me started on this. She posted this list in one of my LinkedIn etiquette groups and credits part of it to Curtise Garner's *New Rules of Etiquette,* published in 2009:

What Not to Do:

- Do not force your way to the front of a line and try to bribe for a table.
- Do not call your server "honey," "sweetie" or other terms of endearment.
- Do not snap your fingers to get the attention of your server.
- Do not snap open your napkin. When seated, place it quietly in your lap, not in your shirt.
- Do not salt and pepper your food before tasting it. To do so is an insult to the chef.
- Do not season a dish that everyone will share.
- Do not cut up your entire meal before you begin to eat; cut a small portion and cut more as needed.
- Do not wipe off silverware when you are eating out. If you discover a utensil that is unclean, ask your server to replace it.

- Do not talk with your mouth full.
- Do not pick your teeth during dinner to remove food.
- Do not reach across people to get to the salt and pepper, butter, etc.
- Do not spit bad food or gristle into your napkin. Remove it with the same utensil with which it went into your mouth, then place the piece of food unobtrusively on your plate.
- Do I have to say it? Do not lick your fingers.
- Do not chew on a toothpick in public.
- Do not lean backwards in your chair.
- Do not lean back and announce "I'm through" when you have finished eating.
- Do not wave your utensils around with food on them while you talk.

So, I asked everyone in the group to share more, and here's what I got:

- Do not slurp drinks or soup.
- Do not lift your pinky finger when holding a drink.
- Do not keep your elbows on the table while eating.
- Do not drink before finishing the bite in your mouth.
- Do not place personal objects on the table such as keys, cell phones, wallets, etc.
- Do not lean on the table with your chest.
- Do not spit olive, cherry, etc., pits.
- Do not yawn or cough without covering your mouth.

- Do not drink from a bottle or can.
- Do not sit at the table with a hat on (men).
- Do not put a hat on the table.
- Do not answer a cell phone.
- Do not disrespect the dress code.
- Do not use your napkin to remove the sweat from your forehead or neck.
- Do not place toothpicks on the table.
- Do not put your dirty napkin on the dinner plate when the server is clearing.
- Never put your dirty napkin on the table until you stand to leave the table at the end of the meal.
- Do not use your hand instead of the napkin to clean your mouth.
- Do not forget to wait until everyone is served before you begin eating.
- Do not make noise with the cutlery and dishes.
- Do not bend toward the plate. Instead, bring the morsels to your mouth.
- Do not sit with your hands behind your head.
- Do not eat with your elbows raised.
- Do not speak loudly to people across the table.
- Do not signal for the server to clear your dish before everyone at the table has completed a course.
- Do not use inappropriate language.
- Do not hold private side conversations at a table with others or text on your cell phone.

Why Is This Important?

I'll summarize with a story that an associate shared with me:

"My beloved grandmother was quite the lady. She taught all of us manners. My uncle was sharing how he was raised and how important manners were to his mother. She would tell him that one day he would be sitting in front of a very important group of people and would need these fine manners. Many years later in his life, my uncle attended a dinner in his honor—he had just become a senator! He looked up to the heavens and thanked his mother!"

While not all of us may end up being senators, there will be important moments in each of our lives when table manners will be imperative to our success or failure in a situation, whether it be large or small!

Formal Dining

Some simple rules can help when dining out at a formal restaurant or at a formal dinner at another person's home. The first rule of thumb is to always show up on time. It's just rude to keep others waiting. The second rule is to smile and be happy without looking fake.

In a restaurant, whatever you are carrying in your hands, such as gloves or a small handbag, should be put in your lap when you sit at the table. (Your hostess or host at a home will normally provide a place for you to store such items.)

Always keep the napkin or cloth on your lap while eating. To avoid the things in your lap from slipping off in a restaurant, put the napkin across your knees, folded diagonally from corner to corner, and tuck the two side corners under, pinning your things in place. If you need to leave the table during the meal, place your folded napkin on your chair seat and push in the chair.

Keep your legs closed rather than crossing them, especially when sitting at the table. If the table isn't high enough, crossing your legs can be uncomfortable.

Don't use your cell phone at the table while you're eating. Put it in silent mode. If you must leave it on, excuse yourself if it rings and go outside or to a private area.

Ladies should never apply makeup at the table. Once again, excuse yourself to the ladies' room. And remember, it is impolite for more than one person to leave the table at a time, regardless of the number of people at the table.

Say "please" and "thank you." Address people with whom you are unfamiliar or who are your elders as "sir" or "ma'am." It's unnecessary to do so when speaking to friends or peers, but don't forget to say "please" and "thank you" to them.

It's impolite to refuse dishes. Take at least a little on your plate and at least pretend to eat some of it, unless you are allergic. And never start eating until everyone is served.

Be sure to follow the direction of the host/hostess. When a dinner has been prepared by a chef who prides himself on being a decorative artist, you may have a problem knowing which part of an intricate structure is to be eaten and which part is scenic effect. The main portion is generally clear enough. If there are six or more, chances are they are edible. One or two of a kind are usually embellishments only. Rings around food are nearly always to be eaten, whereas platforms under food seldom are. Anything that looks like pastry is meant to be eaten.

Don't sit silently and ignore your neighbors at the table—participate in conversation.

Finally, if you have been invited to a restaurant by someone else, do not complain about the food or the service.

And always remember to write a note of thanks, in addition to thanking the host at the end of the meal.

Job Interviews

The Dangers of a Job Interview Lunch

I've narrowed the job down to two candidates that I like. By chance, one is male, the other female. The position is a six-month event production coordinator for an event in New York City. We'll be traveling there a lot, and, of course, this person will interface with the client often.

I want to see how each candidate handles dining out at a restaurant, since the person I select will need to do that on occasion with the client. I'm going to take each candidate on separate days to a quiet, semi-formal restaurant I like in downtown Santa Barbara.

Bob, the first candidate, is already inside the restaurant when I arrive. Oddly enough, he's run into some friends and is engaged in a lively conversation when I enter. He doesn't seem to notice me, so I wait quietly for him to at least be on the lookout for me and do a quick sweep at the front door. Doesn't happen. After several minutes, I walk up and touch his arm. He turns. "John! There you are!" Then back to his friends. "Gotta run. Great seeing you." Then, back to me. "I'm all yours." No introduction to his friends, no "sorry I kept you waiting." Nada.

We get seated, and Bob leans over to the hostess and puts his hand on her arm. "Hey, Sweetie, could you have the waitress bring us a wine list? We're gonna have a glass of wine, right, John? Have to celebrate!" I look at him and smile. "You go ahead; I don't drink." Faux pas number two. Big time.

That doesn't stop him. The waitress arrives, and he orders himself a half-bottle of wine with "sure you don't want any?" I'm waiting to start a business conversation with him, but he immediately picks up his menu and has a conversation about "what to have." Is this the evil twin of the person I saw twice in my office? Or is he trying to illustrate that he's an all-round fun guy who would be great for the client? Unfortunately for Bob, I've worked with these customers for about 30 years, and they're no-nonsense folks. Rather than taking my lead and waiting for me to order, he jumps right in. "I'll have the lobster. This place is known for lobster, right?" *Yeah, it is, but this is lunch* . . . He has the waitress wrap the bib around his neck and is ready to go with a large gulp of wine. Oh, he's polite to the waitress, talks to her like he's interested in taking her on a date and, even after ordering my salad, still hasn't stopped controlling the moment.

I decide to bide my time. When the lobster comes, he begins to break it up with his hands, dip it in butter and make yummy sounds as he devours it, barely wiping the butter from his chin.

Just as I open my mouth with "Bob, let's talk about your ideas for . . ." the candidate holds up a finger, mops his mouth and before swallowing says, "Hold that thought, John." With that, he flips out his cell phone, which thankfully has been on vibrate, and takes a call.

I've about had enough at this point. While he's handling his phone call, I'm rethinking my first impressions of him. He hangs up with "now, what were you saying, John?" With that, he takes another bite of lobster and between swallows comments, "You really missed out by not ordering this lobster, John."

I've had ample time to finish my salad, so I politely use my napkin and put it back on my lap. "Bob, I'm glad you're enjoying your meal." I think to myself, "It's the last meal we will share together." I let him finish his meal with pleasant small talk. When the bill comes, I pay it. As I pay, Bob comments, "Well, John, it was great seeing you! I look forward to our next lunch so we can celebrate our successes in New York with champagne and caviar!"

With that, he is out of his seat and striding over to his friends at a table at the back of the restaurant. I shake my head as I realize he didn't even shake my hand as he left!

While Bob is friendly and does nothing overtly wrong (well, except fail to introduce me to his friends, take a phone call, talk with food in his mouth, forget to shake my hand, etc.), his overpowering attitude when communicating with me is one of *non-engagement*. By focusing on his friends instead of being prepared to meet and focus on the job, he immediately puts me off.

By focusing on the food and wine instead of the job responsibilities, and because of his overbearing interaction with the wait staff, I can't see him fitting in with my sophisticated client.

Fortunately, Barbara, the other candidate, is just what I need. She is immediately attentive and engaged with me. She is polite to the wait staff but focused on my needs and not the menu. She declines alcohol and is more interested in the job and her responsibilities. Her questions are intelligent, and she adds just enough humor to make her an intriguing and successful candidate.

So, next time you're asked to meet a prospective boss for lunch, think about the real purpose behind the meal. With a hiring manager, it's never just about having a meal. It's about how you conduct yourself and whether you have good manners and the right focus while dining.

BUSINESS ETIQUETTE

Is Financial Success Linked to Good Manners?

Recently, an etiquette associate posed the question, is financial success linked to good manners? After that, a lively discussion followed, and Jeanne Nelson, another of my associates, sent me a link to a blog post she had written on the subject last May. I thought this post answered the question so well that I asked Jeanne if I might use it as a "guest post."

Read on to see why Jeanne says financial success is linked to good manners and why the three E's might outweigh the three R's:

A degree is not enough. A study conducted by the Carnegie Institute of Technology has prompted a recent flurry of articles in *Forbes* and other news sources, websites and blogs. According to the study, 85 percent of a person's financial success is due to his or her "personality and ability to communicate, negotiate, and lead," and only 15 percent is due to "technical knowledge." Although the study was published in the 1970s, I'm happy to see it being discussed, because these findings reinforce the need for business etiquette training to enable people to network effectively and build relationships. In other words, it supports the premise that the Three E's—Etiquette, Ethics and Empathy in the Workplace—and Life—are just as important as, and might even outweigh, the Three R's—Reading, writing and arithmetic.

Wait a minute, you say. How can financial success be more dependent on knowing how to shake hands than on how to prepare a financial analysis? How can the soft skills trump the hard skills on which I am spending a fortune to learn in college?

Okay, let's take the medical profession, for example. You want to go to the best doctors, but unless you have dramatic proof that the doctor you've chosen is the best—that is, she was smart enough to remove your diseased kidney instead of the healthy one, or he successfully set your aunt's broken collar bone and she's just dandy now—you're likely to choose the doctor who has the best bedside manner and is most responsive to you. Thus, you've selected your doctor based on his or her personality and ability to communicate rather than on technical knowledge. Regardless of a doctor's sterling reputation, how long would you stay with someone who never listens to you and treats you like you're a piece of furniture instead of a patient who is paying for these insults.

The articles also include further findings that people would rather do business with those they like and trust regardless of quality or price!

Think about it. How often have you preferred the teacher, professor, principal or college president because of his or her dynamic personality, respectful demeanor, loyalty, character or ability to engage an audience? In the community, are you drawn to the banker, pharmacist or car mechanic who greets you warmly, listens to you intently and follows up meticulously on your transactions, or to those who are curt, brush you off and don't seem to be listening to you? The answer is obvious: you'll want to do business with those who treat you as a valued patient or customer, people who seem to care about you and your business and who you like. And aren't you more willing to cut people a break if you like them and have a good impression of them, even if they don't deliver exactly what you wanted?

Does this mean that high school and college no longer matter and that everyone should head off to finishing school instead? Of course not; but what it does mean is that to protect and market those valuable skills you are acquiring in high school and college at great expense to you and your parents (don't forget to count the time you invest as well as the money), you need to ensure that your soft skills are up to par. Envision a pile of gift boxes you have been told all contain the same item; you are more likely to reach for the gift box that has the most attractive and appealing packaging.

The articles further report on:

- Emotional Intelligence (EQ), which allows you to be self- and socially-aware, able to control your emotions and behavior and in tune with others' feelings and needs; in other words, possession of etiquette skills to build your confidence.
- Moral Intelligence (MQ), which refers to your values, ethics, character, honesty, integrity, ability to take responsibility and capacity to empathize and sympathize with others.
- Body Intelligence (BQ), which is the ability to know your body and take proper care of it in order to function at the top of your game.

EQ, MQ and BQ over IQ? And, to round out the alphabet soup as it applies to this topic, I'll add the P's to the Q's that you need to put to good use with those hard skills and valuable experience you are acquiring:

- Prowess—Extraordinary ability to communicate effectively, network masterfully, build meaningful and productive relationships, convince others to see and concur with your point of view and master the fine points of business and social etiquette.
- Power—High level of influence and authority to make important decisions to direct your career and accomplishments.
- Persuasiveness—The skill that allows you to communicate effectively in writing and in person to obtain what you need to fulfill your goals.

To be successful you must be true to yourself. If you are, you will find what you love to do and study to obtain both the hard and soft skills necessary to achieve your goals. Your integrity and sincerity will shine through in your smile, handshake, eye contact, comments, body language and facial expressions and in all the ways you do business. That should be your real goal: getting your E's, R's, P's and Q's all in sync!

Until next time - Jeanne

A convincing argument not just for The Key Class, but for any etiquette training, no matter where you are or what you are doing!

About the Author

Jeanne Nelson is a business etiquette consultant in the New York City area and a former vice president at a Fortune 500 company. To learn more about her and what she does, visit her Web site
http://www.prowessworkshops.com/

<u>Taming the Angry Caller</u>

The phone rings; you pick it up and the voice on the other end begins screaming at you. What should you do? My first thought is to bite my tongue, stay calm and listen. Let the person vent and blow off steam. Don't interrupt . . . even with a solution before he or she tells his or her story. Don't raise your voice. Take it down a notch. Speak softly to show that you're interested in handling the caller's complaint in a calm, rational way.

If the caller is a client and ranting about poor service or an unsatisfactory product, be patient, listen, use phrases like "I understand how you feel." It's important to empathize, never interrupt and apologize. Why? Because that's what the caller wants to hear . . . that you are sorry for offering a poor service or product. However, avoid the words "I'm sorry." Instead, use "I apologize." Why? Because the latter has an air of finality about it.

Let the caller know how you plan to make amends. For example: "I apologize for the inconvenience caused. I will have one of our reps call you in the next 30 minutes. If you'd like to leave your number with me, I'll call later in the day to check on the progress." Always be professional, but let the caller know you're not a pushover.

It's all right to ask the caller to take his or her tone down a notch. Toning it down and speaking softly are the best defenses for tempering a bad mood. Also, slowing down the caller helps him or her think more clearly about his or her choice of words. I'll say, "Would you please repeat that a little slower, because you're running your words together and I'm not sure what exactly you're trying to say.'"

Avoid doing anything to inflame an angry caller further. Most of the time, angry callers have legitimate complaints and have reached the end of their rope. Take the tack of being very empathetic with angry callers. They can sense quickly whether you are a consumer advocate or not.

If someone gets personal or abusive, caution him or her to stick to the topic and try to let you help.

Find value in what the person has told you. No matter what, there is value; this tells your caller that you see value in them and in their message. This, along with following other good listening skills, builds trust and respect and reduces the fear that may be the basis for the outburst.

This is always a great opportunity to fix the problem beyond the client or customer's expectations. When we go above and beyond what is expected, something interesting happens. The customer will often become a more loyal customer, and that loyal customer will share his or her experience with others.

So often it's tempting to place blame on a colleague when dealing with an angry call. The customer does not care who made the mistake. They just want it fixed.

Use the four P's when dealing with a difficult customer or question:

1. Pause—give customers a chance to get all their words out before you say anything.
2. Paraphrase—make sure you know exactly what the problem is.
3. Probe—ask more questions. Dig deeper.
4. Provide response—sometimes, you may not want to provide the response right away, especially if you know the customer won't like the response.

The overall key is to respect the caller, listen and resolve the issue. Never escalate. The results won't be pretty if you do.

You Don't Like My Customer Service Skills?

Have you experienced poor customer service from businesses, restaurant personnel or in retail shops? What are the main reasons we experience poor customer service these days? Does it all go back to training and education? A group of etiquette coaches and customer service experts shared their thoughts with me to provide insight.

Several associates thought the problem was training and education—in part. If it's just having employees in customer-facing roles who do not actually like people, it may be more of a managerial or hiring issue. The point is that anyone in a customer-facing role should really like to work with people. Most of my associates agreed that the challenges that come with dealing with people become too much for someone who would rather be in a back-office role.

Could it be that poor customer service is a reflection of poor self-esteem? "People carry the weight of the world on their shoulders and then transfer this over to others," said Deborah Choma, an instructor at Final Touch Finishing School. To combat this, Choma has a motto that she applies in her own life every day: Be nice to everyone, because everyone is having a tough day. "I have experienced, firsthand, poor customer service turnaround because I was aware of this principle and looked for a way of being kind to them and making them feel good about themselves. Should it be this hard? Unfortunately, it is this hard."

Ruby Syring, a twenty-eight-year veteran of customer relations and specials events at The Boeing Company, offered that the more social media, video games and cell phones children and teens have access to, the more withdrawn they are from face-to-face interaction with people. "This leads to awkward social skills and, therefore, what is perceived as bad customer service," Syring said.

Christine Chen, President of Global Professional Protocol in Washington, D.C., agrees with Syring but believes that there is so much time spent in solitude in today's society that it's not just children and teens. "I see adults who lack people skills due to lack of people interactions. " Chen thinks that poor customer service happens for a number of reasons. "The organization itself has to have a culture of providing world-class customer service. That needs to trickle down to the hiring stage and the training and education of employees. However, the training should not just consist of a one-day session. This needs to be ongoing—daily huddles (even a five-minute meeting), newsletters, communication, refresher courses, etc. I do believe the hiring process should be extremely intentional and rigorous. Too often, organizations hire just to fill a spot. It's better to leave the position vacant in order to find the best person who will take seriously the company's value of world-class customer service."

Teri Haynes of Business Interaction in Shreveport, Louisiana, took it even further. "In looking at the big picture, I think so many of our problems are because of our ME attitude. As a society, we are concerned with ourselves more than with other people. This is reflected in poor customer service, road rage, petty crime, etc. Although we can and should certainly work with adults to develop better manners, starting in the home is the most effective cure. My appreciation goes to all of the etiquette instructors who work with children. Perhaps we should consider developing parental etiquette classes!"

Parental etiquette classes—not a bad idea. What do you think?

Watch Your Behavior in the Workplace!

Mary Abbajay of the Careerstone Group told *Washington Business Tonight* that "bad manners and a rise in workplace incivility are bad for the bottom line." She urged that company managers and leaders need to create positive workplaces.

According to the etiquette experts at the Protocol School of Washington, which trains diplomats and international executives, the top 10 business etiquette missteps are:

1. Using swear words.
2. Neglecting to greet coworkers when you arrive at work.
3. Shouting to others across the room.
4. Declining to offer guests a beverage.
5. Taking calls on speakerphone when others are within hearing range.
6. Wearing unprofessional attire.
7. Offering a weak handshake.
8. Failing to make eye contact.
9. Displaying poor dining skills.
10. Answering cell phones or texts during conversations, meetings and meals.

What Other Experts Say

While these blunders were ranked in the top 10, I decided to poll etiquette experts in my LinkedIn Etiquette & Protocol Group to see what other faux pas we could add. The intention? To draw attention to potential bad moves that might get in the way of business professionals' careers.

Catherine Albertini of the Etiquette and Protocol Institute of Rancho Santa Fe suggested not talking about one's personal affairs too much; this especially includes when men engage in conversations in great detail about their dates with women in front of a woman working in their office. Showing off a photo of your new baby is fine, but personal problems with your spouse or your kid who has croup is a no-no. The more private stuff you keep to yourself, the better. She additionally advised against practical jokes and pranks, which are typically best left outside of the office, as well as sophomoric behavior.

Albertini also indicated that it's very unsettling when one chews gum or sucks loudly on mints or candies. It's especially annoying when one snaps, pops and makes cracking noises while chewing gum. She suggested leaving these items at home.

As far as a professional image goes, we all agreed that too many people show up to work as though they just rolled out of bed into the office, complete with messy hair, dirty finger nails, wrinkled or dirty clothes, messy makeup and bad breath. Unfortunately, image at work is of paramount importance to advancing one's career, and these unkempt workers are neither professional nor on a fast career track.

Didi Lorillard, who runs the Web site, Newport Etiquette and Modern Manners, said she gets numerous complaints on her Web site about coworkers who heat up "stinky food" in the microwave at the office, more so than practically any other office problem. Another thought is not to take what isn't yours out of the refrigerator or leave a mess in common areas.

Lorillard also suggested that if you're working in a cubicle, keep it down. Specifically, don't let coworkers hear you fighting with your spouse. She also advised against having intimate relationships with coworkers. "What happens if you have an affair and it doesn't work out?" Lorillard noted that the most important point to remember is to stay focused and get the job done.

The number one offense for many in the group was coming to work sick and exposing others to their illness.

Jay Remer, The Etiquette Guy, stressed the importance of respecting personal space and boundaries. "These egregious offenses occur both in and out of the office. I find myself explaining to people the importance of protecting one's personal space at all times. Without this respect for oneself, we cannot expect others to have respect for us. The office environment is a somewhat intensified arena where we need to encourage others by example on how to discern when to keep to oneself and when to engage with others."

Several group members commented that the number of businesspeople who do not know how to make a proper introduction is amazing. This is very much a part of making a good first impression.

Terri Fowler, a human resources executive, advised against personal grooming at one's desk. She was particularly emphatic about not clipping nails at work. She advised men not to wear pants that are too short so that socks and shins show when legs are crossed. Another irritant against which she advised men is not to carry and jingle too much change in their pockets.

Everyone agreed that not having management buy-in to enforce office rules, dress codes, behavior and civility policies sets employees up for failure. This is particularly true in businesses where many managers work from home full-time. While common sense may guide most of us, there are those who may be new to a professional environment and unsure of how to act.

Meeting Protocol

April Ripley of The Premier Image Inc. provided some sound inter-meeting protocol tips. "Respect the person conducting the meeting; know when to speak out in a meeting and understand rank—senior officers, bosses and coworkers—during meetings."

Jeanne Nelson of Protocol for the Workplace and Etiquette for Social Situations warned against interrupting people when they are speaking, making a point in a meeting or delivering a presentation.

My personal suggestion? Don't purposely embarrass coworkers.

Gossip in the Workplace

Maybe you think that gossip is a harmless, unavoidable element of corporate life. It isn't. Left unchecked, gossip wreaks havoc on company morale and efficiency. I'm not talking about who had drinks together after work. Rather, I'm referring to talk among coworkers, managers and executives about work-related matters to someone who can't do anything about it. This type of complaining is a way of not dealing with something upfront but handling it in a cowardly fashion instead.

The tendency to complain is human. So why is it a big deal? Primarily because workplace gossip is unproductive, breeds resentment and becomes a roadblock to effective communication and collaboration. This doesn't mean that you should never voice a negative opinion about anything work-related or that you shouldn't be encouraged to question things. But it's ironic that workplace gossip is often about things that really matter to the company or team and should be addressed openly. These include things like:

- Are they going to start laying people off?
- It's not fair that our department's travel-entertainment budget got cut 20 percent while the sales department didn't take a hit.

- I can't believe my boss didn't acknowledge me for my work and took the credit himself!

These things are toxic for the entire organization. When they stop, it means that the team has finally embraced honest communication and is dealing with issues head-on and addressing them to the person who can actually do something about them. This enhances teamwork, trust and good communication.

How Can You Politely Shut Down Gossip?
For this to work, the CEO or senior person has to declare, "No more gossip." A no tolerance policy needs to be adopted. It should be okay for one person to "call out" another, but it needs to be done in a light-hearted way.

To avoid engaging in gossip, steer clear of places where gossip abounds (like the coffee pot) or where people who are likely to partake in it linger. If others start gossiping, change the subject. You can respond with something like, "Oh, I didn't know. So, how do you think the meeting went today?" If the gossiper persists, let him or her know that you are not comfortable engaging in that type of conversation and that you are not interested, and walk away. If you are worried about appearing rude, just excuse yourself to go to the restroom or make an urgent phone call—both legitimate activities during your workday.

Talk to your supervisor rather than a coworker about your concerns. Coworkers may spread your words to others, which will get misinterpreted or exaggerated, thus effectively spreading rumors and gossip. Ultimately, your supervisor will hear a distorted version of your words rather than what you actually said. You don't want to be considered the source of gossip.

Don't repeat gossip to others. If you happen to overhear gossip, don't spread it. Consider reporting the gossip to your supervisor to let him or her know that this is an obvious source of concern within the company.

Encourage those who gossip to go directly to the person who can do something about it instead of simply repeating it to others who have no authority to change it. If you are proactive about avoiding gossip, you can create positive results for your company rather than help deteriorate your workplace.

Remember, if a gossiper speaks badly of another person, he or she will have a tendency to turn around and speak badly about you. Don't trust those who encourage gossip in the workplace. Those who do so often become the destructive force that brings gossip to fruition. This only gives that person power and encourages them to create more drama. Establish yourself as someone who is confidential instead of a gossip.

Are You a Workplace Bully?

Over the Thanksgiving weekend, I spent some time visiting a friend of mine who is being bullied at work. She is experiencing intentional acts that are mentally painful and that are isolating her in her workplace. Even though bullying can involve negative physical contact as well, fortunately, in my friend's situation, that isn't the case.

You might be thinking, "Bullying, in the workplace, really?" Absolutely. Bullying usually involves repeated incidents or a pattern of behavior that is intended to intimidate, offend, degrade or humiliate a particular person or group of people. It has also been described as the assertion of power through aggression. It goes to the mistreatment of those who are not as strong; it also goes to being cruel to others.

Who Could Be a Bully?

A bully can be the boss who uses intimidation and ridicule to manage his employees; a bully can be someone in a position of power who thinks his or her management style is "authoritarian," and that this is the only way to manage workers, when it's really bullying. A bully can be the manager who unfairly or without reason blocks a worker's promotion, refuses requests for leave, reduces or changes shifts, takes away job responsibilities or blocks opportunities for career or job advancement.

Bullies can be the coworkers who bully to enhance their position or sense of power in the workplace; they use overt physical intimidation or subtle gestures like eye rolling to belittle people, especially in front of others. Bullies can be those who get others in the workplace to side with them against a worker or spread rumors about someone's personal or professional life, either verbally or in texts and emails.

Who Is at Risk of Being Bullied?
• Young or new workers or apprentices
• Injured workers or those on a return-to-work plan
• Workers (in insecure employment positions) who worry they will lose their job if they complain (this is my friend's situation)

What is the Effect of Bullying in the Workplace?
Bullying doesn't just affect the victim's personal health and well-being. The overall workplace will often experience increased absenteeism, lateness, lost time and staff turnover. Disciplinary or conduct problems will occur. Teamwork will suffer and most likely a decline in respect for management will result because of its allowing bullying to happen. This, in turn, will generate a negative public perception of the organization and its ability to attract workers. Finally, this will lead to inefficient, disrupted or reduced productivity.

What Can You Do If You Think You Are Being Bullied?
If you feel that you are being bullied, discriminated against, victimized or subjected to any form of harassment, there are specific steps that you should take.

In my friend's case, the bullying is happening with a middle manager, along with some of her "pet" employees. Here's what I advised my friend to do:

- FIRMLY tell the person that his or her behavior is not acceptable and ask him or her to stop. You can ask a supervisor or union member to be with you when you approach the person.
- Keep a factual journal or diary of daily events. Record:
  o The date, time and complaint in as much detail as possible.
  o The names of witnesses.
  o The outcome of the event.
  Remember, it's not just the character of the incidents, but the number, frequency and, especially, the pattern that can reveal bullying or harassment.
- Keep copies of any letters, memos, emails, faxes, etc., received from the person.
- REPORT the harassment to the person identified in your employee policy, your supervisor (or his or her manager) or a designated manager. If your concerns are ignored, go to the next management level.
- DO NOT RETALIATE. You may end up looking like the perpetrator and will most certainly cause confusion for those responsible for evaluating and responding to the situation.

Bullying is an unkind act that no one should have to endure. If you experience or witness bullying, take steps to eliminate it from your workplace.

Office Cubicle Manners

You're sitting in your cubicle at work busy with a client proposal for the boss. A shrill, irritating cell phone ring pierces the air and interrupts your train of thought. The person in the next cubicle over answers in a loud voice. Suddenly, you hear him jump to his feet and start cursing and screaming. It's the worst! He's rude and inconsiderate beyond belief, and you've spoken to him about it before. You put on your headphones and turn on some music to block the noise, and you wish you had one of those sound-proof cubicles you've heard about. You make a note to ask the boss in your next meeting.

The cubicle world is just the place to show off incredibly poor etiquette! This isn't just a once-in-a-while event but a daily annoyance. Some of the worst behaviors include:

1. The loud person whose every word either on the phone all day or to others literally hurts your ears. You cannot hear yourself think and you cannot hear your own phone calls.

2. The chronically ill person who is always sneezing or hacking up a lung but will not wash his hands or take a sick day.

3. The "over-sharer" who stops by frequently to tell stories about her personal life that you wish you could wash out of your brain. This can happen several times a day because there are no doors. It doesn't matter if you ignore her.

4. The person in the next cubicle who pops his head up into your space just to see what you're doing.

5. The frequent eater who loves food with onions, garlic, fish, pepperoni, etc., at her desk.

6. Loud personal radios—worse if he sings along.

7. The person who talks to herself out loud all day.

8. The chair squeaker.

9. The "love bug" who must talk to or have visits from the object of his desire that you must either hear or witness.

10. The snoop—the person who goes through the files and drawers of others when they are not around.

What Should You Do?

The positive side of cubicles is that they promote teamwork and collaboration by not cutting people off from one another. But the poor manners of cubicle inhabitants sometimes overcome the positive effects. If you haven't already, suggest to management that they institute some simple rules for employees. For those that can't be handled by management, take some initiative.

1. Management should ask everyone to keep their telephone voices in a moderate range. Explain that loud conversations interrupt the workflow of others and thus lower overall productivity.

2. The company should encourage people who are sick to use leave days and not to come to work until they are no longer infectious. Ask them, when they do return, to use hand sanitizers, wash their hands frequently and not to leave dirty tissues lying around. Perhaps management should encourage letting employees work from home when they are well enough to work but still dealing with the residual illness.

3. From a one-on-one viewpoint, tell the constant over-sharer that you are too busy to take a break and then turn to your work hoping he or she will get the hint. If the person doesn't take the hint, politely explain to him or her that you will only be able to talk during breaks. Ignoring the over-sharer when he or she comes around will eventually send the right message.

4. Management should require that employees take lunch in the lunchroom or out of the office. It's better for employees to take a break, even a short one.

5. The company should request that employees keep all radios at a low volume.

6. If someone frequently talks or sings to himself or herself and it disturbs you, respectfully tell him or her that it bothers you and to please stop. If the person ignores you, speak to your supervisor.

7. Offer to use a can of WD40 on your neighbor's squeaky chair!

8. Ask your boss to speak to annoying love birds in the office and ask them not to disturb others with frequent visits. If they continue, tell them they are disturbing you. This goes to a matter of wasting time and productivity, and management should be able to handle it for you.

Meeting Etiquette 101

This article by Dan Janal, author and PR expert, will help you increase your etiquette IQ so you don't make a fool of yourself at your next meeting, conference or convention. Note: all these stories are true. Dan says he couldn't possibly make this up.

Meeting Etiquette 101
The people you meet at meetings and conventions are the friendliest, politest and most considerate people in the world. Except when they are crashing boors!

1. If you want to have your picture taken with a celebrity while he or she is talking to someone, DO NOT interrupt the conversation, ask for a picture and run off with a thank you to neither the celebrity nor the photographer. This happens so often you wouldn't believe it. DO THIS: Wait patiently for the conversation to end, introduce yourself politely, ask to have your picture taken and say "please" and "thank you" often to the celebrity and the photographer.

2. If you are talking to someone beneath your exalted status in the hallway, DO NOT look over the

person's shoulder and look for a more important person to talk to. DO THIS: End the conversation politely at an appropriate point and leave the person feeling like he or she had a meaningful interaction and was not cast off in favor of a bigger fish.

3. Do not sing in the elevator. Ever. Ever. Ever. Yes, this did happen to me as the elevator doors opened on the 30th floor and I stepped into the elevator to see and hear a woman singing an original song that sounded like "I don't love you. You don't love me," which she repeated several times. She didn't stop when I entered. I quickly realized that 30 floors can be a very long ride, and as I leapt out of the elevator as the doors closed, I heard, "And I know you don't love me." I continued hearing it for some 20 floors as the voice grew fainter and fainter.

4. If you want to talk to someone who is talking to someone else, DO patiently wait off to the side and join in at an appropriate moment. DO NOT barge into the twosome and immediately interject your thoughts. These people were having a conversation. Just because you want to network doesn't mean you have permission to barge into someone else's conversation.

5. When someone starts a polite conversation with "What do you do?" that is not an invitation to give a twenty-minute, nonstop sales pitch for you and your topic. DO NOT consider this an invitation to go

into great detail about your personal issues with drugs, abuse or health issues. DO give a fifteen-second blurb that positions you and DO ask the person what he or she does. Remember that it takes two people to have a conversation, but only one person to be a bore.

About the Author

Dan Janal, author of Reporters Are Looking for YOU!, helps small businesses get publicity so they can sell more products. His clients get terrific results from his coaching, consulting, done-for-you services and do-it-yourself tools. For more information, visit www.prleadsplus.com or call Dan Janal at 952-380-1554.

How to Break Up with a Client – Part 1

I just read an extremely interesting article written by Rae Robinson, a freelance writer who sent me some information. In it, she gave me a link to her article "How to Lose a Client in 10 Days." This was of interest because I recently spoke to a few associates who told me they'd love to "lose" several clients but don't want to offend or have a confrontation with them.

My advice to them was just what Rae told me, "Sometimes your happiness, not to mention your success, depends on breaking up with clients who are holding you back."

Interestingly enough, her article talks about how to fire a client without burning any bridges. In fact, she said that the ex-clients would not only be fine with being left but would also be inspired to give out glowing testimonials or referrals!

Wow!

The first step, she says, is to write the first draft of an email letting the client know you're going to have to move on. Next, she provides some tips:

• Be short and to the point
• Don't give too much detail—they can ask for it later
• Be professional, not emotional

• Say that you will continue for two weeks or until they find a replacement, whichever comes first

Even though Rae's message is for copywriters, her information can apply to any market. So if you've been thinking about breaking up with a client, go to:

http://www.awaionline.com/2012/05/how-to-lose-a-client-in-10-days/ to learn more about how to do it!

Read Part 2 to learn how not to burn the bridges you've built when firing a client!

How to Break Up with a Client – Part 2

As I discussed in Part 1, the key to breaking up with a client is not to burn bridges. Don't just break up with the client, give him or her something first.

Here's what I did with one client, and it was in tune with Rae Robinson's advice in Part 1. This occurred in my event production business. Let's call the client Alan. He started working in a variety of niches that I didn't enjoy. When I told him I was ending our business relationship, he was upset. I was a cool, collected cucumber, all business, just like you'll be. He immediately attacked and told me I wasn't going to find clients if I wasn't willing to work in a variety of niches.

In many industries, professionals who specialize make more money and are happier with their work. But most people don't realize this. So I told Alan that there were clients everywhere who would be willing to pay top dollar for his services if he was willing to niche himself, look for those clients and ask for the fee he deserved. He walked away from our conversation not only fine with the fact that I was breaking up with him, but excited about the future of his business too.

That's what I call a smooth breakup! And it's because I gave him something in return.

The benefits of the breakup were tangible immediately. I was no longer stressed out. I didn't dread checking my email. I had energy to work with my other clients. It was absolutely the right decision.

So, here's your task for today:

1. Come up with something you can give your client. It might be knowledge. You might offer to train or find your own replacement.
2. Write your email. (If you've always communicated by phone or some other manner, use that medium—but write down what you're going to say.)
3. Walk away from your email for a few hours, look it over again and revise if you need to
4. Then . . . send it!

Tell your client you will finish any projects you're already committed to doing if he or she still wants you to.

And, of course, be confident. You've already decided that this is what you must do for the growth of your business. This is your life!

<u>Generations in the Workplace</u>

Sometimes Gen Yers rub older, more experienced colleagues the wrong way because they are eager to take on responsibilities, prove themselves and do things differently. More experienced colleagues often become resentful when managers agree to Gen Yers' demands for rapid advancement or special accommodations and rewards. However, the most frequent complaint from older, more experienced associates is that they believe Gen Yers do not accord them an appropriate degree of respect and deference. At the same time, Gen Yers sometimes feel they are treated with disrespect by older, more experienced employees.

Jeanne Nelson, a business etiquette consultant, has spent many years hiring, training and supervising Generations X and Y as high school interns and has created a series of workplace-readiness workshops to help them adjust to corporate culture. According to Nelson, "Young people come into the work environment convinced that they are ready to set the world on fire, only to see their aspirations go up in smoke once they realize that there is a structure and process with which to deal. They run into that brick wall called WCRP, or *workplace culture / readiness / politics.*"

How can managers help Gen Yers avoid this problem?
Bruce Tulgan of RainMaker Thinking, Inc. suggests the following. "First, remind them that their older, more experienced colleagues are older and more experienced. Consider assigning each Gen Yer an older, more experienced person as a peer adviser. Although the peer advisers may have no official authority in the relationship, the peer adviser role creates one-on-one relationships of trust and confidence and mutual respect between Gen Yers and their older colleagues. It is very important that these relationships not be pro forma, but rather that a concrete business purpose, such as training, be attached to the relationship.

"Next, if you assign special responsibilities, award fast-track promotions, or make accommodations or rewards available to Gen Yers," says Tulgan, "then you should make a serious effort to make them equally available to older, more experienced workers too. Any special treatment should be available to older and younger workers alike and always in exchange for meeting clear, measurable performance expectations."

Today, many companies have orientation programs geared toward welcoming and indoctrinating Gen Y hires into their particular corporate culture. The workshops Nelson created and conducted at her company helped to incorporate students into the workplace culture. But these programs only work if managers are also on board and have a template for dealing with the generational differences.

Nelson also emphasized that "companies have been intimidated by the hype of the Millennial Generation and have tried to mold their company policies to fit the expectations and demands of Gen Y instead of expecting Gen Y to fit in with the company policies. But some companies apparently have turned instead to hiring older workers, as shown by a report a couple of years ago that indicated that during a certain period, the hiring of older workers actually surpassed the hiring of new grads in Westchester County, New York. There is a belief that older workers are more experienced and reliable on nearly every level. And, despite the perception of many to the contrary, older workers' technology skills are just fine and get the job done."

Nelson suggests that it's important to put the technology thing into perspective. "Although Gen Y grew up on the cutting edge of the Internet age, the Boomers grew up on the cutting edge of the computer age and are not exactly clueless. Steve Jobs, the Gen Y role model, was a Boomer after all! And, since the first Gen Yers are now in their 30s, they should be looking over their shoulders at Gen X (the current crop of high school students and undergrads) coming up behind them with even more tech savvy to compete for jobs."

The bottom line? We all truly need each other and have to be willing to find a way to work together for both our collective and individual success.

About Jeanne Nelson and Bruce Tulgan

Jeanne Nelson is a business etiquette consultant in the New York City area and a former vice president at a Fortune 500 company. To learn more about her and what she does, visit her Web site:
http://www.prowessworkshops.com/

Bruce Tulgan of Rainmaker Thinking is an author and speaker. His bestseller, It's Okay to be the Boss, and his blog articles can be found at
http://www.rainmakerthinking.com.

Let's Throw a Party! – Holiday Office Etiquette

Eight Professional Image-Building Tips for the Holiday Office Party

The annual office holiday party can be a wonderful opportunity to solidify relationships with the boss, coworkers, direct reports and others. But for some reason many people think this is a time to let down their hair, dance on tables, swing from the chandeliers and tell their bosses what they really think of them. Still, the holiday office party is an ideal professional networking opportunity and should be treated as such.

With that in mind, here are some guidelines to help you build your image and make the most of your holiday office party.

#1 – Don't drink too much; better yet, don't drink at all! Careers, reputations, credibility and relationships that have been built up over time can be sunk in an evening because of actions or comments at the office holiday party! Alcohol impairs one's judgment and loosens one's tongue—a disastrous combination. Offending someone with an off-color joke, letting slip a confidential piece of company information, sharing a nasty piece of office gossip, making unwanted sexual advances, dancing on the table or blowing in your boss' ear can cripple or end your career with the company.

#2 – Remember your dining etiquette. Haven't we all seen people who eat directly from serving dishes on the buffet table, pile their plates so high they resemble The Cat in the Hat, pick food off another's plate, talk and laugh with their mouths full or carry on conversations over the heads of others while standing in the buffet line? Don't be one of those people. It's not about the food; it's about connecting with people in a positive way.

#3 – Dress appropriately and tastefully. You're not out clubbing with your friends; you're with colleagues, your boss and possibly clients.

#4 – Don't show up without RSVPing or bring an uninvited guest. This is particularly important if you're attending a sit-down dinner. Understand that a holiday business event is not a place to bring your children.

#5 – Don't criticize the food or music to your host or others. Criticizing how you are being entertained is the very worst of poor manners. Be appreciative of the effort made on your behalf.

#6 – Don't bring up contentious issues. If someone gets out of hand, lighten the mood by light-heartedly changing the subject. Saying "Let's go grab a piece of pie!" or pulling people out on the dance floor with some good music are possibilities. If the offender is particularly obnoxious and the host doesn't notice, let him or her know so the behavior can be appropriately handled.

#7 – Don't tell dirty or racist jokes. Most etiquette experts agree that there should be zero tolerance for these types of comments. It's the host's job to make everyone comfortable, but it's also acceptable for another guest to let the offender know he's crossed the line. Quickly swing the mood of the party back to everyone having a good time.

#8 – Have fun. This is the end-of-year celebration of everyone's hard work. Just remember your manners and conduct yourself with wit, warmth, respect and dignity.

This article was run in the WE Magazine for Women Holiday Gift-Giving Guide for 2012. To read the entire issue, go to http://bit.ly/WEGIFTGUIDE2012.

Business Gift-Giving Tips

According to the National Business Association, corporate gift giving should be done in a professional manner. When your company makes the decision to incorporate a corporate gift- giving policy, there are a few things to keep in mind:

1. If you are giving a corporate gift to a client or potential client, always check with his or her company to ensure that it allows corporate gift giving.

2. Corporate gift giving should never be used to compensate clients or employees for less-than-expected wages or services.

3. Corporate gift giving should include personal gifts, as this tends to offend some clients or employees.

4. Corporate gift giving should comply with your company's budget. Do not go overboard and buy gifts that you cannot afford or try to save money by purchasing gifts that are "cheap," like ink pens or toys that last about an hour.

5. Corporate gift giving should make recipients feel good about their accomplishments. Give gifts that cost about the same price across the board.

6. If your company uses corporate gift giving as a holiday gift, make sure to check the recipient's religious or cultural background.

7. If you prefer to give corporate gifts in person, you should always check recipients' schedules to ensure that you are coming at a good time for them.

John J. Daly, Jr.

ETIQUETTE IN GENERAL

Rules of Etiquette

Whether for business or social purposes, I find that the following four rules of etiquette are often ignored.

1 Opening the Door—Any Door

As late as the 20th century, a gentleman always opened doors for ladies. Whether it's the lady they were driving or a stranger entering a building, it was always the correct thing to do. This has almost entirely vanished and is not entirely the fault of men. I've witnessed women sneering at men for opening a door for them. They seem to be confusing manners with chauvinism. My advice in this case is to smile at the sneering lady and open the door anyway.

2 Writing Thank You Notes

In days gone by, after winning new business, completing a professional transaction or receiving a gift, a person would write a thank you note as soon as possible. Socially, this was appropriate even if the giver was a relative. Parents would sit children down after a birthday or Christmas and coach them on their first thank you notes. Unfortunately, in today's world, gift giving has now become an obligation, and the idea of a thank you note is long-forgotten. Teach your children to write thank you notes, whether for receiving gifts or for potentially showing appreciation for business-related opportunities. If you do, they'll have a greater appreciation for what others do for them.

3 Arriving on Time
In days past, it was rude to arrive late—for anything. "Fashionably late" was a nonexistent term. Lateness was rudeness—always. If you were invited to dinner and arrived 15 minutes late, you would most likely end up eating alone in the kitchen surrounded by household staff. You would then only be allowed to join the party when the polite guests (who arrived on time) had finished and were retiring for the evening's entertainment. Think about it. If you're late for dinner, an appointment or any other engagement, you're wasting other people's time.

4 Returning Phone Calls
One of my biggest irritations is with people who don't return phone calls. Even if you don't have an answer to the caller's questions, always return calls. Take the time to let the caller know what you're doing to get the requested information, or direct them to the appropriate place to get it. If you're going to be out, have someone pick up your calls, or at a minimum, have your answering system tell the caller when you'll be able to return the call.

When you initiate a call and get a receptionist or secretary, identify yourself and tell him or her the basic nature of your call. That way, you'll be sure you're getting the right person, and the person you're trying to reach will be able to pull up the appropriate information and help you more efficiently.

When you're on the receiving end of a phone call, identify yourself, and, if the call is business-related, identify your department. Answer the phone with some enthusiasm or at least warmth, even if you are being interrupted. After all, the person on the other end doesn't know what you're doing.

Top Modern Etiquette Trends

While networking, I found the following piece written by fellow etiquette coach Elena Neitlich. I liked the wisdom in it, and, with Elena's permission, I wanted to share it with you.

Top Five Etiquette Trends Going Into 2012
By Elena Neitlich

In the past couple of years, etiquette has been a hot topic and has enjoyed lots of visibility in the news media. Following are the top five etiquette trends going into 2012.

One: More and more impatience. The world continues to move faster and faster, especially online. Expect people to want instant answers and to get impatient and upset when they don't. Worse, if it's so easy to get things done via the Internet and smartphones, expect people to get ever more impatient with other human beings. So, be more aware of expectations, and remain polite when things are delayed.

Two: More foolish postings online. Kids, teens and adults have more and more forums to post information (and pictures) online and damage their reputation. Remember to practice discretion—both online and off.

Three: More and more places to see bad behavior. Politics, reality television, YouTube, sensationalized stories in the media—all of these continue to grow in popularity while serving as atrocious examples of behavior. The world needs people to reset the bar and serve as role models for polite, civil discourse and habits.

Four: Rudeness while multitasking. Many people seem to be doing five things at once: checking email, talking on a cell phone while typing on the computer, eating lunch while preparing a report. When we multitask, we are not focused on making others feel comfortable and respected. Sometimes, as when someone drives while texting, multitasking can become downright dangerous. Treat others with civility, giving them attention and being present for them while interacting.

Five: More people on edge. We are living in challenging times. Many people are already upset and seem to be almost looking to get into arguments. It is essential for all of us to develop good communication skills and to know how to keep situations from spiraling into serious arguments.

The spirit of etiquette is the same as always and will never change. It's always about making others feel welcome, comfortable and respected. It's about a certain lightness of spirit, caring and empathy.

About the Author

Elena Neitlich is the owner of Etiquette Moms. Learn more by visiting http://www.etiquettemoms.com.

New Tech—New Rules?

Not long ago, my wife and I went out to a very nice restaurant to celebrate our anniversary. As we sat reminiscing about the wonderful life we have shared over the past 29 years, we heard a shrill ringing behind us. The ringing was so annoying that I turned to my right to see a lone diner answering his cell phone in a booming voice. He proceeded to have a long and loud conversation. He discussed his daughter, who was suffering from anorexia, and his ex-wife, with whom he obviously had shared a life similar to that portrayed in the movie *War of the Roses*.

As sad as it may seem, all conversation stopped in the restaurant while *everyone* listened to this terrible one-sided phone call. Every now and then one guest would look at another and just shake his or her head. It wasn't until the profanity started that I became really upset with what was happening. And, of course, there wasn't a wait person to be found, so I couldn't even mention my concern. At last, our server brought our salad to the table, and I asked if there was something that could be done about this rude and disrespectful man. The waiter disappeared, and we all continued to suffer through the loud string of profanity.

Soon, the restaurant manager made an appearance, and several diners simultaneously asked him to speak with the man about his conversation. Of course, as you might imagine, when the manager approached him, the culprit became belligerent and indicated that he didn't understand. "What's the big deal?" he said. He went on to say that he was a lone diner and could have been having the same conversation with a dinner partner. Finally, after another rude comment into the phone, the manager asked him to stop his conversation or take it outside. This was followed by a reply into the phone summarizing how expensive the place was and how he was being harassed. Then he finally hung up.

What was the man thinking? Why would anyone want to share the information he was letting out with a roomful of strangers? What right did he have to interfere with people's enjoyment of an evening dining out?

Along with the convenience of cell phones comes a responsibility to be considerate of others. When we lose that simple code of living in society, we are on our way down the wrong path.

If you are in a public place, put your phone on vibrate. Unless you are a doctor or expecting a baby within the next hour or have a true family emergency, refrain from answering calls. If it is a must to answer the call, do the polite thing and ask the caller to hang on for a moment while you get yourself to an isolated place where you can speak. Try to take the call outside. If that fails, try the restroom, which, by the way, is not the best alternative, since talking in the restroom can also create a disturbance. Remember, just because the phone rings doesn't mean you have to answer it.

The same goes for constant texting on a cell phone. When you are face-to-face with someone, give that person the respect and consideration he or she deserves. Respond to text messages when you are alone. Texting in front of someone is the same as sitting with someone and ignoring them in favor of another person. Don't do it!

Rudeness – Today's Top 12 Rude Behaviors

Peggy Post's 17th Edition of "Etiquette" outlines the following as today's rudest behavior!

1. Telling racist or ethnic jokes, which not only insults the listener's intelligence but smears the entire conversation.

2. Using foul language and other obscenities in public without any reservation—especially in the presence of children.

3. Doing the "cell yell"—conducting a cell phone conversation so loudly that those around you are staring at you.

4. Treating a salesperson, food server or any other service provider as someone who is beneath you.

5. Letting kids run wild or make constant noise in restaurants, supermarkets, theaters or any other public place.

6. Endangering others on a busy expressway by playing NASCAR: zipping from one lane to the other

while driving crazily and not bothering to signal (this actually frightens people).

7. At a youth sporting event, abusing the referee, coach or opposing team's players.

8. Fouling the sidewalk with spit, trash or pet poop.

9. On public transportation, staying planted in your seat when an elderly, pregnant or disabled person obviously needs it.

10. Charging thoughtlessly through crowds—especially when skating, riding a bike, riding a motor scooter or pushing a baby stroller.

11. Butting in, whether jumping into a checkout line in a store or taking a parking space for which someone else is clearly waiting.

12. Lighting up to smoke tobacco in a roomful of nonsmokers—and failing to ask permission beforehand.

How to Handle Rude People

The boss raises his voice and loses his temper. A coworker is unsupportive of your requests. A client uses her authority as a push factor to get things done. A manager is continually disrespectful. These are tough situations. How should you handle them?

Why Are People Rude?

First, let's look at some of the reasons why people are rude. It's much easier for people to be rude over the phone, on the Internet or over email. Why? Because rude people often feel disconnected from others. That's why they lose it over petty things that won't matter in the next hour. Because they feel disconnected, in their minds, they have no reason to change that feeling. And when they're face-to-face with you, they have no idea why they should behave differently. While the golden rule should always apply, it often doesn't.

People often are rude because they are having a bad day, and misery loves company. Always remember that it's not your fault. Sometimes you can divert that bad mood by remaining calm and joking about something small. This often brings out the rude person's need to vent, and in that case, you should just listen. This means overlooking the rudeness and just talking to them. Perhaps they don't have anyone else they can talk to, and you might just leave them feeling better.

Some people want to intimidate you into submission to make themselves appear stronger. It's the bully syndrome. Bullies are weak on the inside but don't want to show it. These are disconnected people. If you face them head-on, they often back down. This doesn't mean you become the bully, but rather that you face their behavior with them. The method is to "State, Inform and Request." View this short video to see how it works: *http://www.5min.com/Video/Learn-how-to-Respond-to-Rude-People-142081094.*

Famous people like Simon Cowell have built their celebrity on being rude. Watching rude celebrities has become a national pastime. Again, these people are not connected with other people and only have an inflated sense of self. If we stop supporting the rude behavior of celebrities, they'll get the message. The same goes for people at work or in business who are chronic about rudeness. Stop enabling them.

How to Handle a Rude Coworker

- Don't lose your cool
- Don't take it personally
- At the first occurrence, give the benefit of the doubt—try to cheer them up or be a good listener (as indicated above)
- Take it away from others; suggest grabbing a cup of coffee to discuss the issue privately to clear the air
- If the person refuses to take it out of the workplace, say, "There's no reason to be rude; what is the problem?" This will make the rude

person think and sometimes results in his or her walking off and pouting.

- If your authority or position is being challenged, take the opportunity to privately get to the bottom of the issue. Ask, "What have I done to upset you and cause your rude behavior toward me?" Keep a good sense of humor about yourself. Don't get personal. Keep it businesslike.

If the boss explodes at you, remain calm and respectful. Look him or her in the eye and request a meeting to discuss the issue. This applies if you are in a public meeting. When you meet, be both firm and pleasant. Discuss the issue, explain your position and aim for a solution. Always repeat the resolution back so there is no misunderstanding. If you have done something to upset him or her, provide assurance that you will correct these issues so that there will be no reoccurrence. Be sure to let the boss know that you view his or her exploding at you as a very disrespectful situation and that you feel it damages your reputation and self-respect.

I'm Walking Here!

What side of the sidewalk should we walk on besides the sunny side? Seems like a pretty simple question, but it creates confusion for a lot of people. I've been asking people to send me their biggest pet peeves when it comes to etiquette and social graces. The question above seems to be an ongoing concern. People feel frustrated when they run into each other just trying to make it down a busy sidewalk. Oddly enough, this is not such a problem in one of the busiest cities in the world, New York. New Yorkers are very accustomed to walking everywhere and have learned the correct way to do so from childhood. The quick answer to the question: Follow the same rules as the flow of motor traffic, no matter on which side of the street you are.

Gentlemen, please walk on the curb side when walking with a lady or an older gentleman.

How Did this Tradition Start?

So where was this tradition initiated? During early civilization, before they were paved, roads were almost always pitted mud holes that also served as the sewer system. Passing carriages would splash mud onto the sidewalks or boardwalks. It was also the custom in those early days before plumbing for people living on the second stories and above to throw waste from their windows into the street. This included garbage as well as human waste. They would do their very best to have everything land in the street, but often the waste would hit closer to the curb, also splashing those using the sidewalks. This is why gentlemen walked to the outside. I would bet this is why so many wore hats, so as to protect their ladies' dresses from being splashed. This tradition has survived in many places but has gone by the wayside in others. However, I will make a guarantee to gentlemen—when you do walk on the curb side, ladies will notice. They may not mention it, but their opinion of men who practice this simple courtesy will go up a few notches.

A simple gesture while walking with an elderly person is to offer your arm or hand while navigating a curb to cross the street or in a very crowded area.

Nosegays

Another custom that was born during those early times was for ladies to carry small clusters of fresh flowers in a tight grouping called a nosegay. Ladies held these flowers to their noses as they made their way through the streets because the smell from the gutters was often very offensive. The flowers made their noses happy, or "gay," as it was referred to in those days. This tradition carried over to many weddings and persists even to this day. Gentlemen, if you really want to make a hit with a lady, pick up a small bunch of flowers for her before a date!

<u>Texting While Walking</u>

Yes, I was in a hurry this morning. The line at Starbucks was out the door, and the guy in front of me took forever to decide on the three drinks and pastries he wanted to purchase. But I prevailed and got my venti extra shot latte. While I was carefully taking a sip as I exited the door, a guy with his face buried in his iPhone barreled into me as he furiously texted. The coffee scalded me and ruined my nicely pressed shirt. His apology? "Hey, Dude, watch where you're goin'!"

Excuse me? It took all my good manners to avoid an altercation. I felt like punching the guy. Now I'd have to go home, change my shirt and be even later than I expected for my morning appointment. But I bit my tongue, wiped myself off and changed shirts.

According to a *New York Times* January 8, 2012 article, while there's little current data about the number of people injured while texting, more than 1,000 pedestrians visited emergency rooms in 2008 after they were injured while using a cell phone to talk or text. That number has doubled each year since 2006, according to a study conducted by The Ohio State University. I shudder to think about that guy walking into traffic or falling into a hole. And what about innocent pedestrians like me? I have a burn on my chest the size of Nevada.

162

Navigating the sidewalks of any major city can be as difficult as playing football at times. But when your opponents are walking while texting, they aren't watching where they're going. That can obviously make a two-block walk to Starbucks both maddening and life-threatening at the same time!

Let's gain more control over our increasingly electronic lives and stop acting like zombies with our BlackBerrys and iPhones replacing eye contact, handshakes and face-to-face conversation. Let's live in the present, be where we are and stop existing in cyber land.

Email Etiquette

Most people are unaware that they might be sabotaging their career success with poor email etiquette.

All technology issues aside, people do business with those they trust. Building trust depends on consistently making a good impression through personal interactions, phone calls, texting, email and social media. For now, let's focus on email.

If you're communicating with family and friends, your email style should be informal, as if you were having a casual conversation. On the other hand, formality is the rule of thumb for business and professional emails. You only have one chance to make a great first impression, so your email must convey your "intended message."

As the song from the iconic television series *M*A*S*H* says, "Suicide is painless." It's particularly easy to commit professional suicide by email! Here's how to avoid it:

• Use a targeted subject line.
If you're like me, you get hundreds of daily emails, and the subject line might be the deciding factor on whether to open it or not. For example, use "Here is the quote you requested for the Porsche presentation" instead of "Here it is."

• **Make reading your email as easy (or painless) as possible.**
When you can, use bullet points and subheadings to separate different sections of your message.

• **Try to keep the email less than 25 lines.**
Use short paragraphs and only address one topic per email.

• **Don't create an email with multiple topics.**
It's much too frustrating to respond to three or four topics within a single email.

• **Use bold formatting to highlight the most important points in your message,** such as the first sentence of each paragraph or first point in your bulleted list, as I have done here.

• **Proofread your work before you hit the send button.**
Do not rely on spell check.

• **Do not use emoticons, graphics or colored backgrounds in business emails.**

• **Avoid using acronyms like BTW (by the way) or LOL (laughing out loud).**
These should be limited to informal emails to family and friends.
• **Edit the subject line when replying.**
The nature of the email may have a different context.

• Always use a proper salutation.
This can be "Dear Mr. Daly," "Dear John," or "Hi, John" if you are on a first-name basis. Don't be informal and use a first name with someone you have never met.

• Use a formal closing.
"Sincerely" is a good formal closing. Acceptable semi-formal closings include "Best regards" or "Warm regards." Your signature should include how to contact you. If you want to include a one-line marketing phrase, you may do so. An example might be, "How 21st Century Manners make a difference." But don't make it a brochure!

• Don't send negative emails.
Always try to be positive and create the impression that you are a problem solver, not a problem maker!

• Avoid using the "reply all" feature.
This generally causes more harm than good!

• Use the out-of-office message.
If you are unable to return emails while you are away, this will help others understand why you are not responding to them. Don't forget to turn it off when you return though.

• Don't use all caps in an email.
This is the equivalent of yelling at someone!

If you follow these simple rules, you'll discover that people will respond to you readily and in a more positive manner!

<u>Standing in Line</u>

Sharing a Medical Diagnosis with Strangers

It's 8 a.m. and I'm late for work. The line isn't too long. The woman near the front of the line turns to the stranger behind her. Suddenly, she begins to confide about the large fibroid tumor she is having removed the next day. What this has to do with getting coffee is beyond me. She goes into detail, saying it's the size of a grapefruit and weighs 30 pounds! She's so enthralled with her description that she fails to see that the barista is calling out "Next" to her. I try to nod toward the counter, but she is waving her hands and pointing to her stomach. Her description is so loud that her voice fills the shop. I'm confounded as to why she would share this with a roomful of strangers rather than a close friend. Perhaps she has no one else? What do you think? Should the person she was talking to have said, "It's your turn," and nudged her forward?

Talking on a Cell Phone in a Grocery Line

I am in a grocery line of about four people. I'm next in line. Another clerk opens up a new register. The woman talking loudly on her cell phone at the end of my line sprints to the newly opened register. That should have been my spot, so she's being kind of rude. A little common courtesy for fellow shoppers would have been appreciated. But she's probably thinking, "Hey, it's every person for himself; too bad." Then she proceeds to stay on the phone, talking about what a despicable person her ex-husband has become. She gets emotional and turns her back on the register, forcing the clerk to remove all the items from her cart. She can't even put the phone down long enough to pay her bill. She juggles the phone and constant conversation with the credit card reader, taking up more than her fair share of time to check out. Then she strolls slowly out, pushing her cart, still on the phone. Still waving her arms, she walks into traffic in front of an SUV, whose driver slams on the brakes to avoid hitting her. It doesn't faze her. She doesn't even notice because her cell phone conversation has now totally consumed her. Do you think she would have sued the SUV driver if he'd hit her?

Chatting it up with the Bank Teller

It's lunch hour. I decide to run to the bank. I'm at the back of the line with eight people in front of me and only one window open. The person at the window is processing a lengthy transaction, of course. But, more importantly, once the transaction is completed, he continues the ongoing monologue he's begun with the teller about his week, the inconvenience of having to provide all this information to the government and lord only knows what else. Those in front of me shift from one leg to the other, trying to contain their impatience. He's unperturbed and hardly aware of the long line behind him. The teller glances apologetically at the next person in line, but he totally ignores her cues and finishes his conversation with the air, since the teller has stopped acknowledging his comments. Finally, after what seems like five or six minutes, he turns but doesn't acknowledge the long line, now quite lengthy, as he leaves.

Self-absorption has become rampant in our society. Do you think the teller should have let him know that the lengthy line behind him needed her attention and told him to have a nice day instead of letting him go on?

Do you think these circumstances warrant the polite interception of others? Let me know what you think!

Apologies – What to Do with Unaccepted Ones

What does one do when one apologizes and the offended party will not accept your apology? I was scratching my head on this one when Deborah Choma, an associate and instructor at Final Touch Finishing School, told me about Leland R. Beaumont's book *Emotional Competency*.

She pointed me toward the "elements of an effective apology" in the book. According to Beaumont, an effective apology addresses specific needs and omits important ones. While the emphasis will vary for each situation, this is helpful information to keep in mind when apologizing. Beaumont says that a successful apology will include each of the following four elements.

Offering an Apology

1. Accept personal responsibility; acknowledge the specific offense and the pain it caused and clearly take personal and unconditional responsibility for the offense.

2. Acknowledge directly to each of the injured parties your role in causing the damage and their suffering.

Show remorse and humbly and sincerely describe the painful regret you feel for committing the offense. Look backward to express your regret. Then demonstrate forbearance by looking forward to describe the lessons you have learned and the changes you have made to ensure nothing like it will ever happen again.

3. Offer an explanation; honestly, candidly and simply describe why the offense happened. If it was inexcusable, simply say so.

4. Make reparations; fully repair the loss if possible. Otherwise, ask: "Is there anything I can do to make this up to you?"

Accepting an Apology

If you receive an apology, you can choose to accept it, ignore it or reject it. If the apology contains all four elements described above, Beaumont says, it makes sense to accept it. Even if the apology is lacking in one of the elements, it is sensible to accept it if it is sincere, if it demonstrates remorse and if the relationship is worth maintaining.

Forgiveness can be a strength. However, if the apology is inadequate and you believe the omissions are deliberate and manipulative, turn down the apology and give your reasons for doing so.

Beaumont insists that "an apology that lacks authentic remorse is seriously deficient and deserves to be declined. An off-handed 'I'm sorry' is rarely adequate. When declining an apology, it is best to describe what you see deficient in the apology, referring to the four elements above as the standard for an acceptable apology."

When you DO accept an apology, be gracious and sincere without any attempt to insult or humiliate the person apologizing. Do not exploit the vulnerability exposed as the person apologizes. Use this as an opportunity to strengthen the relationship and not as an opportunity to inflict harm.

"Power shifts are apparent when offering and accepting a sincere apology," Beaumont says. "Acknowledging a wrong exposes vulnerability, but choosing to apologize for it demonstrates strength. Having the option of accepting or rejecting the apology creates some amount of power, and this may transform the victim into the powerful one. The decision to accept or reject an apology may depend partly on the history of the power relationship that already exists between the two parties."

Do you think this is much ado about nothing? Then you'd be wrong. Refusing to either apologize or accept an apology can have devastating results for both parties. Think about it.

Deborah left me with a parting thought to share. "Believe that a transformation is achievable for every individual. Our manners are a compass that points us to succeed."

Tips for Air Travel

What are the deadliest etiquette sins committed during air travel? Whether traveling for business or pleasure, alone or with the family, the challenges and discomfort of the process are exasperating! There's check-in, arrival and departure delays, baggage handling (and loss), airline seating in tight quarters, irritating and officious airport and airline personnel, being trapped on the aircraft sitting on the tarmac for hours, poor or no food and anxiety over terrorist attacks. No wonder people on all sides of the equation are grouchy, irritable and rude!

Here's the result of being trapped inside the pressure cooker of an airport or aircraft and taking it out on your fellow travelers:

- Talking loudly on a device that has become an extension of your hand.
- Cutting in line.
- Pushing and shoving.
- Speaking rudely to other travelers.
- Piling large suitcases in front of people in line.

- Taking seats on the aircraft that are not assigned to you.
- Climbing over other passengers repeatedly.
- Fidgeting in your seat and constantly bumping the seat in front of you.
- Complaining about a crying baby.
- Not doing everything you can to quiet the crying baby.
- Not doing everything possible to keep children quiet, occupied and comfortable.
- Allowing your children to bother other passengers.
- Being demanding of, snapping at, arguing with and speaking rudely to flight attendants or pilots.
- Stubbornly refusing to follow the requests and instructions of airline personnel.
- Speaking loudly to your seatmates and traveling companions.
- Repeatedly pressing the button to summon the flight attendant.
- Taking up more space in the overhead storage bin than you are allotted.

- Shoving your too-large in-flight luggage under the seat in front of you to the discomfort of the passenger in the seat.

- Snoring, gagging and coughing without doing something to alleviate it.

- Spreading out in your seat to the discomfort of your seatmates.

    If you are guilty of any one of these transgressions, think about how your actions would cause you discomfort if directed toward you. Are your actions thoughtless or do you really want to be viewed as rude and uncaring?

Honoring Elders

Monica Brandner, CEO of *The Etiquette Princess©*, recently posed a question: "Why is teaching our children to honor their elders important?" She went on to discuss how, over the past 30 years, our society has seen a separation in the family unit due to divorce, moving across the country and conflict between children and their parents. As parents age, they tend to want to be closer to their families, a desire that isn't always realized.

Consequently, our children don't always have much in common with their grandparents. But here's an area where we can all learn to teach our future adults how to show kindness and respect to others. Monica came up with four simple etiquette tips to help us honor the "Golden Generation."

You might ask why I would include this in a book devoted to business etiquette. The answer is quite simple. All adults learn from their parents, whether intentionally or not. Parents lead by example, either positively or negatively. Therefore, when we become adult professionals, the respect we have for others has grown from the examples our parents have set with our grandparents.

Here are the four tips Monica formulated:

ATTITUDE – Model respectful behavior your children can imitate. Smile, give a hug and laugh. Help your children see what it looks like to enjoy the elders in your family. Grumbling and complaining releases bad attitudes in our homes and gives our children permission to think poorly of others.

ACKNOWLEDGMENT – No one likes to feel like they are invisible! Have your children look their grandparents in the eye and say, "Hello, Grandma and Grandpa."

THANKFULNESS – Being thankful and thoughtful is like giving a mini gift! Coach your children to say "please" and "thank you." Teach them how to be appreciative of the gifts their grandparents give them and not just to expect them. Have your children draw pictures on a thank you card, because grandparents are usually thrilled to receive them and it engenders children's creativity while teaching them to think about others.

TIME – Surround your family with seniors. To bridge the gap of genders at family gatherings, have your little children put on a play, sing a song or dance for their grandparents. Having fun builds bonds!

Finally, one of my personal tips: If the grandparents are physically up to it, arrange for them to babysit or take vacations with you and the kids so they'll have more time to be together and understand each other. It was on a vacation when my grandchildren were about four years old that we truly bonded together.

These are simple, easy-to-do suggestions. Take the time to show our future adults how to treat others respectfully. When they're grown, they'll make great business owners, managers and employees. Think about it. It all starts at home.

Monica Brandner is the co-author of Sarah Elizabeth Plans a Tea Party, CEO of The Etiquette Princess and President of Image by m. brandner. To learn more about her, visit www.etiquetteprincess.com and www.imagebymonica.com

Give Up Your Seat!

The woman seated next to a window looks like she might deliver her baby at any moment. A young, athletic-looking woman of about 20 is sitting next to her in the aisle seat. The bus stops and an elderly man who looks to be in his 80s slowly climbs onboard, but there are no seats available.

The very pregnant woman offers the gentleman her seat. There's just one problem. The young woman next to her refuses to move over to the window, and the gentleman is physically unable to crawl over her. He motions to the pregnant woman to just sit back down. The young, athletic woman is selfish and unbelievably rude.

At the next stop, the athlete gets off the bus, and finally the elderly man sits in her seat. At the same time, a woman on crutches gets on, and the elderly man rises to offer her the seat. However, the pregnant woman stands and moves into the aisle, allowing the woman on crutches to sit as the elderly man slides over to the window seat.

As the bus moves forward, the heavily pregnant woman hangs on and looks around to see if some able-bodied person might offer her a seat. No such luck. Everyone meticulously avoids eye contact with her and leaves her standing for the next several blocks, where she exits the bus at the next stop.

The kind pregnant woman didn't make a stink about standing; she didn't want to ask others to give up their seats. But if you see someone less physically able than yourself on a bus or train, don't you think the right thing to do is volunteer your seat? If someone asks you to give up a seat or move over to accommodate someone, why wouldn't you be willing to do so? Isn't this really about respect for others?

By law, the seats nearest the door are reserved for the elderly and those with disabilities, when necessary. If you're in one of those, it's imperative to give up your seat. Think of it as a way to stay active and, therefore, healthier. Don't make people who are potentially in pain or having an extremely difficult time just moving around suffer when you are perfectly capable of standing. Think of it as a *random act of kindness!*

Have you performed random acts of kindness lately? What do you think? Have you had any bad (or good) etiquette experiences on buses or trains?

Pet Peeves about Poor Manners

Not too long ago, I asked my friends on Facebook to send me their "pet peeves" about poor manners. I kicked if off by pointing out that disrespect is mine, because it fuels so much bad behavior. Here's what I got back from them.

- People who don't pay attention. People are so "wired-in" they can't be present and pay attention to the people around them!

- Folks who are so focused on what they need to do that they are oblivious to the negative impact their behavior is having on others. Just try taking a trip to the local supermarket to see this in action. How many times have you seen someone leave a carriage smack in the middle of a two-lane aisle as though no one else in the world needed to use the same two lanes? The worst thing is to then have to draw their attention to the fact that you or someone else cannot get by. I'd love to see people get beyond themselves and their agendas to be more aware of how their actions impact others.

- Those who humiliate or criticize others, because it destroys the relationship.

- People who wear baseball caps in a restaurant while eating; people who hover over their plate and shovel in food; people drinking from a glass while chewing food.

- Drivers who don't use their turn signal while driving.

- Women who wear heavy perfume and people who are close talkers.

- People who have a hard time being considerate of other people without some direct or immediate benefit. Whether it is cutting in line or cutting someone off in traffic, I often wonder how these people feel or behave when they are treated with the same lack of consideration. Perhaps the real issue is that they lack empathy or the ability to put themselves in other people's shoes.

- My pet peeve is people not taking responsibility for what happens in their lives. It's always someone else's fault that they didn't get the promotion, etc., instead of taking responsibility for their own actions and behavioral issues.
- The top two bad behavior problems are: 1. ingratitude, and 2. disrespect. The effect is the attitude present in today's society at large. I cannot say anything much worse of a person than that they are not thankful to those who have been their benefactors.

- I would say profanity. Profanity occurs when people have reduced their own self-respect and self-discipline. As respect and self-discipline decline, the door is opened for other disrespectful and undisciplined behaviors. I have found that when children and teens are trained to speak without profanity, they display a higher level of respect for themselves and everyone around them. Very interesting "domino effect."

- My top pet peeve is a person who is a liar or a cheat. It's the epitome of a lack of consideration, respect, trustworthiness and any semblance of social skills. The absolute worst would be violent or abusive behavior, which likely stems from a lack of having a conscience. These are all traits of sociopathic behavior.

Foul Language

I was reading a perfectly good article in the *New York Observer* until I hit the "f word" and cringed. You see, my mom taught me that using profanity shows a person's lack of vocabulary! She taught me that if I couldn't express myself without it, particularly in public, then I'd be considered rather uneducated. I'm not sure what is behind the mentality that says it's appropriate to curse . . . in public. I'm not denying that I'm guilty of cursing, but never in public or where it would be inappropriate.

Harassment

Part of the problem is that profanity has become too commonplace in our language. As great as the offerings on cable TV are, they have opened the door to such language, and it's only become worse over the years. The language people use in their own homes is their choice, but to make it public is another form of pollution! In a manner of speaking, it's a form of harassment.

Additionally, topics of conversation that used to be taboo in public or mixed company are bantered about like a discussion of the weather forecast. To those guilty of this level of bad taste, it is profoundly annoying.

Why Do People Use Foul Language?
Often it's because people are frustrated and want to be heard. They think if they use profanity, what they're saying will spark attention. This has led me to believe that those who use extensive profanity feel that others aren't listening to them!

Others use foul language as filler, for the shock value and because of their lack of vocabulary. They also think it sounds "cool," especially if they are young men. They think it makes them fit in or sound more mature or brave or tough. I would imagine the only people who might be impressed are other young men who are doing the same thing!

Unfortunately, using profanity quickly becomes a habit that is hard to break, and that in itself can be very damaging. For example, I know some highly qualified professionals who are respected for their technical expertise, but their regular use of profanity damages their brand and limits their career advancement.

A teacher friend indicated that she told her students there are some 500,000 words in the English language and to get creative and use something different, even if they had to bring back a word that has been retired! She also shared that her daughter did that when a man insulted her. She asked if he thought she was a "trollop." It shocked him so badly that he was speechless. Needless to say, he didn't insult her again.

Need some good words? Try *The Thinker's Thesaurus* to find obscure words to use in communications.

On another note, it is far from impressive when someone uses profane words in an article. It shows an extreme lack of self-respect and very low self-esteem. It is disrespectful to others and definitely will not help one get promoted.

Resulting Negativity

Anyone who continually uses foul language quickly becomes unpleasant, often making those around him or her uncomfortable. These people become a "heavy load" and can often be labeled "energy vampires." This will stunt anyone's ability to move ahead in his or her career.

Root Causes

Much of this is attributed to upbringing and the environment our parents create for us and the subsequent paths we choose to pursue. This is a reflection of our times and our value systems and what has been accepted by the mainstream. Whereas once children were being punished for cursing by having their "mouths washed out with soap," these days kids are suing parents and alleging abuse, leaving us with a generation of kids that feel "untouchable." Thus, this behavior has become mainstream.

Profanity isn't only rabid among our youth, but with adults too. And, unfortunately, these adults are the ones left to "lead by example."

In the final analysis, foul language use is a case of people not knowing how to express themselves and not understanding how profanity offends others.

<u>Good Manners: The Good, the Bad and the Ugly about my Voice</u>

I can't begin to tell you how much trouble my voice has gotten me into, while at the same time bringing me so much success. How is that possible, you ask?

The Good

Think about it. I have a big, booming voice. On top of it, I'm very passionate about that to which I devote myself. Picture me standing in front of an American audience or a client, arms waving all around, painting word pictures of what I'm describing, getting excited, joking, playing with the audience. My passion for what I'm selling is very open. I've been told it's infectious. People in America, fortunately, like this about me when I'm teaching, lecturing or selling, and it has brought me success.

The Bad and the Ugly

Outside of America, my voice has gotten me into trouble. Now, trust me. I'm not an Ugly American. Really. I'm just forceful and enthusiastic. But that enthusiasm wasn't so much appreciated in Asia or France when I first arrived there during my event production days.

Let's start with when I was working in Asia. People would cower because I would be talking and using my hands and being so demonstrative, and then, when I was done, I'd want to give them a hug! All the while, they were thinking, *Who is this maniac? He's loud, throwing his arms around, and now he wants to hug me?* I appropriately learned to tone it down, but it was a rude awakening when I first arrived there.

In France, I went into a furniture rental store to secure $200,000 in rentals. This wasn't Asia; it was France. The French are passionate people, right? Uh, not at the pace I was on. I was waving my arms, saying, "I'll take this, and this!" The poor proprietor thought I was nuts. Finally, my interpreter pulled me aside and whispered, "If you want to win him over, calm down, sit down and have a little wine, cheese and bread with him." Ah, another lesson from a different perspective. A good one. Life is to be enjoyed, not rushed.

What Does This Have to Do with Good Manners?

Let me tell you another story to try to connect the dots.

A friend of mine, an event producer, was traveling in Nashville, Tennessee, with an associate from New York. (New Yorkers are notorious for their fast pace and wanting quick answers and results.) The two of them were trying to find a farm venue. They soon got lost, and the irritated New Yorker stopped and approached an elderly man sitting in his front yard with his bloodhound. "I'm looking for the McCormick Farm. I know it's here! Supposed to be there somewhere!" She glared at him, tossing her head in a direction farther down the road. "We can't find it!" she reiterated. At this point, she was almost yelling at the gentleman.

The man looked up at the New Yorker from his chair and quietly said, "Well, ma'am, 'fraid I can't help ya."

At that point, the New Yorker, who was driving the car, stomped back to her companion and sped away, throwing rocks up on the gentleman's front lawn. They drove around for another half hour and still couldn't find the McCormick Farm.

My friend finally convinced the New Yorker to return to the gentleman's house. This time, my friend approached the gentleman and said in a Southern accent, "Hi, I like your dog." She then scratched the bloodhound's ear and continued. "Say, we've been looking around. Beautiful country."

"Yes, ma'am. Been here 70 years." The elderly man smiled at her.

She smiled back and politely asked, "Could you help me? We were trying to find the McCormick Farm, but we've gotten lost."

The man smiled again and offered, "Go up to the next road to the right, turn and go about 400 feet, and then make another right, and you'll be on the McCormick property."

My friend smiled back. "Thank you so much. By the way, how old is your dog?"

The answer was prompt. "He's 14. Want a glass of lemonade?"

There it is . . . going back to manners. We must use the proper code of behavior for the specific *situation* in which we find ourselves. That's etiquette. That's manners. Do you see what I mean? It's all about consideration for other people and how they will react to you. If you show them consideration, they will do the same for you, and you will find ultimate success!

A VARIETY OF THOUGHTS

A Nation of Togetherness

America has been a nation focused on helping and improving the lives of others. According to Alixe Mattingly, Vice President of Communications and Marketing at the Santa Barbara Foundation, this focus has been with us since the very first pioneers traveled west. Mattingly told me that many historians believe the earliest examples of volunteerism in America began when colonists had to form support systems to survive the multitude of challenges that came with relocation. This spanned from farming the land to overcoming devastating illness. "Togetherness," Mattingly says, "was vital for survival, and that lesson was not only learned but remembered by future generations."

Communities thrive when people join together for causes in which they believe. Santa Barbara, California, has been a bright example of how volunteers have made a positive difference in the community. So many people give of their time and talents to causes that matter to them, and they do so in a variety of ways. With the downturned economy, the need is even greater today. And people are working to provide food to those hit by the recession, enabling transportation for the elderly, helping keep the arts alive and mentoring our young.

In that spirit, the Santa Barbara Foundation has created a short film that captures the spirit of volunteerism that was shown during The Man and Woman of the Year Awards on September 15, 2011. I was honored to be a part of the film because of my work with The Key Class.

Because there are so many unsung heroes in the volunteer work I do, I wanted to take some time to thank two of them: Isaiah Ornelas, former Assistant Brand Manager of The Gap* at Paseo Nuevo, and Jill Shalhoob of Jill's Place, both of Santa Barbara. Isaiah, Jill and their companies have provided endless support to The Key Class.

An entire class is devoted to teaching my students how to put the appropriate outfit together for job or college interviews. Isaiah provided numerous combinations which students selected and tried on in order to get the appropriate "look" for interviewing. Isaiah and The Gap provided their support for a number of years, and I couldn't work as effectively as a volunteer with teens without them.

Students have proven what they've learned at Jill's Place on each final night of the course. Jill and her company, Jill's Place, provided at-cost meals to me so that students could undergo the final "live-action" exam and prove that they could display the social manners necessary to impress a prospective boss or recruiter. This wouldn't have been possible without Jill's generosity and caring nature. She, too, has helped me for several years. When I try to thank her, she always wants to know, "What else can I do? I want to help even more!"

It's caring hearts like theirs and so many of my other friends that make us a great
nation of togetherness! I'm honored to know all of you.

To view the Santa Barbara Foundation video on volunteering, visit
http://www.thekeyclass.com/a-nation-of-togetherness/.

*At this writing, Isaiah Ornelas is currently working with Macy's, which also works with The Key Class in the same manner as The Gap! Our hats are off to Macy's as well!

Why Would I Want to Volunteer?

What better gift can you give than helping others? Volunteers most often get back more than they give while helping others. From personal experience, I can promise you that you won't regret it. I've been volunteering for more than 20 years, and it has enriched my life in countless ways. I understand more clearly how I want to live my life, and I have a deeper knowledge of those whose lives are far different than mine. Volunteering has made me more tolerant, compassionate and, more than anything, respectful of others.

The Results of Volunteering

Because I have been a mentor to young people for more than 15 years, I have discovered the importance of the skills I teach for **The Key Class**. Here's how it evolved. A number of years ago, I took a young mentee to a restaurant, and he ordered chili. I sat in horror as he began to eat it with his hands. I quickly asked him to stop eating. "This isn't going to work for me," I interjected. "Please go to the restroom and wash your face and hands." While he was gone, I quickly set up all the utensils and the napkin he would need, and when he returned, I demonstrated to him how to correctly eat chili. He finally looked me in the eye and said, "Thank you, Mr. Daly. I didn't know any of this. Please teach me more."

That was the day I decided to create **The Key Class**; my volunteer efforts had opened up a whole new career for me. I was already involved in a profession that included coaching corporate personnel in business etiquette, so it became my goal to teach young people all the expected social manners, particularly those that affect their getting a job or successfully passing a college entrance interview. My reward? Working with hundreds of students to change their lives. And believe me, that is more important to me than anything else I could ever do. I can't even begin to express how pleased I am when a student rushes up to me on the street and says, "Mr. Daly, I got my job because of what you taught me!" Or the calls just to say thanks at Christmas time. Just recently, I was honored as the Goleta Valley California Chamber of Commerce Volunteer of the Year for my work developing The Key Class!

It's nice to be appreciated, but the work volunteers do is an even better reward. Try it; you'll see!

Think about what you can do throughout the year to help others.

Ways to Volunteer

- Help an elderly neighbor by taking out his or her trash cans or helping with the lawn.

- Spend some of your holiday time at soup kitchens for the homeless. You can donate food items, pick up donated food, serve food, prepare food or offer administrative assistance.
- Participate in holiday toy drives.

- Volunteer at the hospital. You could sit at reception and greet people or deliver flowers to patient's rooms—every hospital is different and needs volunteers.

- Help out at school. Schools always need help with reading to children, assisting on field trips, preparing bulletin boards or just helping the teacher. You'll have to go through a background check, but that's a good thing because it keeps criminals and predators away from children.

- Be a mentor (my favorite). Not every child has a perfect home life. There are those who have only one parent or who live with grandparents or even foster families. Mentoring a child can make an amazing difference in his or her life. Organizations such as Big Brother or even the Boys and Girls Club are excellent ways to volunteer as a mentor. Again, you will have to undergo a background check before you can volunteer as a mentor, but it's all to keep the children safe.

- Work at church. Most churches don't turn a profit, so they rely heavily on volunteers. You can volunteer at church by offering to work in the daycare room, teach a Sunday school class, organize a church function, clean the church and much more. Contact an official of the church to find out how you can help.

- Deliver meals. Most communities sponsor a Meals on Wheels service, which involves volunteers delivering meals to the elderly. Not only will you deliver a hot meal, you will be offering the warmth of companionship to elderly people, who are sometimes very lonely individuals.

- Help with hospice. This isn't for everyone. It can be emotionally draining. If you do decide to do this, you may be the one person the family of a patient relies on. This might involve visiting patients or family, offering childcare or running to the grocery store. Basically, you will be doing simple tasks that wouldn't get done otherwise.

- Work at an animal shelter. If you're an animal lover, this could be for you. Animal shelters are always looking for people to walk dogs, feed the animals and clean up after them as well as find them forever homes.

- Foster a pet. Animal rescue groups need people to foster pets until they can find forever homes. In addition, many military personnel need people to take their pets while they are in service. What a rewarding way to volunteer for the community, particularly if you live in a military town.

- Get involved with Coats for Kids. This organization strives to ensure that every child who needs a winter coat receives one. If your area doesn't already participate in the Coats for Kids Foundation program, think about starting one! To find out more, visit *www.coats-for-kids.org/*.

Remember, one person can make a difference! Take one or several of the various ways to volunteer in your community listed above and get involved. It will do wonders for your self-esteem and give you clearer insight into how you might want to live your own life. And you will help others in more ways than you can know!

The Basics of Networking

Do you have to push yourself to go out and meet new people? Would you sometimes rather be alone? All of us have felt that way from time to time, but in order to get a job or grow your current business, it's necessary to get out of your comfort zone and actively network with others to secure job or client contacts.

If you could use a bit of help in this area, or if you could just use some tips for connecting with new contacts, I wanted to share the following list of networking tactics compiled by John Wood at American Writers & Artists, Inc.

1. Take advantage of your local chamber of commerce.
   The chamber of commerce in your area most likely stages ongoing events where you can meet local businesspeople. Most chambers have a core group of regulars who will introduce you to people and make it easier for you to network. Businesspeople will be impressed with your initiative to seek out potential employers. If you are looking for clients, this is a great way to build relationships.

2. Become a member of a business networking association.

The three largest of this type of organization are Ali Lassen's Lead Club, LeTip International and Business Networking International (BNI). In his book Endless Referrals, Bob Burg says that BNI has generated more than 3 million leads (or over $1 billion in revenue) for its participants. The purpose of these groups is for members to introduce other members to leads for their business—this way, you are never in a "cold-call situation." What a great way to research potential businesses if you are looking for a job.

3. Join an association related to your niche.
   Depending on your niche, chances are there is an association that's been set up to represent and assist its members. One of my long-time friends was fresh out of college when she joined an association in which I was active. She volunteered for projects, networked like crazy and got to know everyone. After getting work with numerous other members, she met her current business partner, and they have been in business together for 20 years!

4. Go to conferences, exhibitions and product launches.
   It makes sense to go where your target audience will be. If you're a job seeker, always be on the lookout for events that target the businesses at which you would like to work. Even if you only attend one or two a year, it can have a significant impact on your contact list. If you're looking to work for Internet marketers, you might want to

attend a conference geared toward Internet marketers, and so on.

5. Take training courses.
   Aside from increasing your expertise in a specific area, training courses are a good way to meet businesspeople or potential clients or people who will refer you to potential clients or employers. For instance, if you are trying to jumpstart a career in writing, take classes taught by literary agents or publishers so that you can begin a relationship with them. This will come in handy once you have written work to sell.

6. Use Meetup.com.
   A quick and easy way to find local business events in your area, you can use Meetup.com to find both business and entertainment events. Simply type in "event planning," "production," "networking" or whatever else interests you in the "Topic or Interest" box, insert your zip or postal code, click the search button, and you'll have a list of groups in your area that are available to join.

7. Join a speed networking group.
   The concept of speed networking is based on the concept of speed dating. You need to have your elevator pitch down pat. It needs to get to the point quickly and convey what you can do for others. Example: "I'm a graphic artist. I assemble images, typography or motion graphics to create a design piece primarily for published, printed or electronic media, such as for brochures, advertising and web design." Then you'll need a stack of

professional-looking business cards. It's advertised that you can get more contacts in one night than most people make in a month. Google "speed networking" to find a group in your area.

8. Participate in online communities.
   Exchanging ideas and making contact with people online is a convenient and easy way to gain new contacts. In as little as 15 minutes a day, you can actively participate in LinkedIn groups and discussions on other business-related sites. This is a great way to quickly raise your profile in your industry. Participate in message board discussions, comment on blog posts and keep active on Facebook. It only takes one good contact to make it all worthwhile.

9. Join community service clubs.
   If you've been meaning to help out in the community, a good way to do so is to join the local Rotary, Lions or Kiwanis Club. You might even want to serve on one of their committees. These are not venues to actively pursue a job or promote the services you offer, but they're still a good place to meet the movers and shakers in your community who could one day play a role in giving you your dream job or boosting up your business.

My next entry will show you how to be a good networker whether you are introverted or not!

About John Wood
John Wood is a freelance writer affiliated with American Writers & Artists, Inc.

<u>Would You Believe Listening Is the Best Networking Tool?</u>

You don't need to be a social butterfly to be a good networker. All you really need is to be a good listener! Get people to talk about themselves by asking questions and just listening. They'll think you are one of the sharpest people they've ever met. It's true! People love to talk about themselves!

Bob Burg's book, *Endless Referrals*, helped me put together eight tips you can use at your next event to ensure you meet all your networking goals.

1. Take the initiative by introducing yourself.
   When you get the chance, Burg says to identify and then introduce yourself to people he calls the "Center of Influence." These are people who are longstanding and active members of the community, and who in all likelihood know and can introduce you to people you will benefit from knowing.

2. Use Burg's "can't miss" networking questions.
   Burg recommends using what he calls "feel good" questions. These are questions that are not

"probing or sales oriented in any way." Because of this, they are perfect to use at a networking event where your goal should not be to sell or talk about yourself. In fact, when networking, your goal should be to learn about the other person. As we all know by now, people are most interested in themselves.

Here are Burg's ten questions:
- How did you get started in the widget business?
- What do you enjoy most about your profession?
- What separates you and your company from the competition?
- What advice would you give someone just starting out in the widget business?
- What one thing would you do with your business if you knew you could not fail?
- What significant changes have you seen take place in your profession over the years?
- What do you see as the coming trends in the widget business?
- Can you describe the strangest or funniest incident you've experienced while running your business?
- What ways have you found to be the most effective for promoting your business?
- What one sentence would you like people to use in describing the way you do business?

3. The most important question you will ask at a networking event.
    The whole key to networking is not to act like you're just there to find a buyer for what you sell. If you're too pushy or give a nonstop sales pitch,

you'll quickly turn people off. The best way to network is to take an interest in and help other people. After you get to know someone a little bit, the one question to ask that Burg says "separates the pros from the amateurs" is "How can I know if someone I'm speaking to is a good prospect for you?" This question immediately tells the person that you could be an important contact for them. Plus, it takes full advantage of the "Law of Reciprocity": if you help someone else, they will want to return the favor.

4. Remember and use people's names.
    It goes without saying that it's important to remember people's names. If you can't remember the name of the person with whom you are talking, he or she will think you're not interested enough in them to make the effort. A person's name is music to their ears. A networking technique Burg suggests using after you meet someone is to go back to them later and use their name. You're bound to make a big impression on him or her. The other person may have forgotten your name already, but he or she will make a point of knowing who you are from that moment on.

5. Introduce people you meet to each other.
    By doing this, you start to become a "Center of Influence." After you introduce people to each other, explain how they could possibly benefit each other. If you've asked them both the above "most important question you'll ever ask at a networking event," you'll be able to suggest to them how to identify people who are likely prospects for their

services. Remember, it's all about giving. If you do it enough and sincerely, good things are bound to happen to you.

6. Give people your business card.
    The number one purpose of giving people your business card is not so that they have your business card, but so that you have theirs. Once you have their contact information, you can use it to refer business to them, send them articles that might interest them and generally keep the relationship going.

7. Give people your complete focus.
    When you're talking to someone, give them your complete focus. Nothing will stop a relationship from flourishing quicker than if the other person gets the impression you're not really listening to them. Ignore what's going on around you and give the person you're talking to your complete attention.

8. Think of networking as a fun adventure.
    Attitude is everything in life, especially when you're in networking mode. If you look at networking as something you "have to do," you might as well stay home. Always think of it as an exciting and fun adventure, and you'll do just fine.
    How will you know if you're doing a good job networking?

Burg writes in his book:
"If you are networking correctly, the other person will never notice you are networking."

What great advice, something we can all reach for. Remember, people don't like to be sold to—they like to buy. If you can come off as the solution to one of their problems in a non-sales, consultative way, there's a good chance it will be an easy decision for them to hire you.

About Bob Burg

Bob Burg is an author and speaker best-known for his book Endless Referrals. Over the past few years, his business parable The Go-Giver (coauthored with John David Mann) has captured the imagination of readers. He regularly addresses corporations and associations internationally, including Fortune 500 companies, franchises and numerous direct sales organizations.

Effective Communication

I asked my best friend and long-time associate Andrea Michaels to provide me with a guest blog. She is an amazing businesswoman, writer and human being. Read and learn from her:

I grew up in an immigrant household where English was not even the second language. Little did I know that I would be able to embrace life lessons in manners and etiquette from what at the time I found to be an unwelcome experience. My parents were Holocaust victims new to the United States after WWII. My mother was Croatian; my stepfather was German. Each spoke a multitude of languages . . . none of them English. Their friends were European, and they did not assimilate themselves into U.S. culture at all. So poodle-skirted girls and crew-cut guys were not my milieu. Oh, no, I was expected to "dress to the nines," even when I went to the mailbox! I'm talking hats, gloves, dresses, stockings . . . not what most teenagers in the 1950s wanted to embrace.

Learning to Navigate between Two Worlds

You're wondering what this has to do with etiquette, right? I, the child, lived in an American world by day and a foreign world by night and weekend. I had to work at understanding the language and innuendoes of two different cultures. It taught me to listen carefully to words, tone, body language and the subtle meanings behind all of those. It taught me to be quiet. And when I spoke I learned to speak clearly and slowly and not to use big words or words that had double meanings. I aimed for clarity. I learned not to use my hands, not to raise my voice, to look someone in the eye when I spoke to them, to pause in-between sentences (to make sure they understood) and to wait patiently for responses before continuing to talk.

In addition to language, I had to pay attention to cultural differences. That meant religious observation, dietary restrictions (you've never lived until you've served up a shellfish platter to an Orthodox and Kosher family), political leanings and not arguing when I disagreed. Again, it was respect for others.

My Reward

This has paid off because my clients are almost all from other countries. I have been privileged to teach throughout the world to people who speak no English, though I do not speak any other language. How do I make this work? Because I speak slowly and clearly and allow time for translation. I use simple words to express myself, and this illustrates that I honor the listener. I do not expect others to speak English or understand my U.S. culture. I know that when I travel, I am the one who must adapt. In the same way I respected my parents and their friends, I feel that I owe it to all those who influence my life to respect who they are in their entirety.

It has stood me well.

About the Author

Andrea Michaels is the President of Los Angeles-based Extraordinary Events, an award-winning international meeting and event planning and event production firm. The company is currently listed by Special Events magazine as one of the "Top 50 Event Producers in the World." Michaels is also the author of Reflections of a Successful Wallflower – Lessons in Business; Lessons in Life and has coauthored several other books. She is a frequent guest speaker at conferences and meetings throughout the world. To learn more about Andrea Michaels and her company, visit www.extraordinaryevents.net.

Changing Your Attitude

When you can't change your circumstances, adjust your attitude!

Bruce Tulgan (http://www.rainmakerthinking.com /blog/) wrote the following on his blog:

"This young woman who worked in our office was always coming in moping around here," I was told by a manager in a medical devices company. "She always had an excuse. Her personal life was always out there. Bad days for her were bad days for everyone. Ironically, if you tried to talk to her about the fact that she was leaving early or moping around, she'd freeze right up. Even if I tried to say, 'I know you locked your keys in the car; I know you had to go to Cleveland; I know your uncle is sick, but you really can't leave until your shift is over,' she'd turn around and tell me in this cold, harsh tone, 'My personal life is none of your business.'

"The manager continued, I finally sat down with her and said, 'Listen, it's up to you whether or not you want to share your personal issues with people here at work. But you need to do that outside your work time.' I told her, 'Your personal life is your own business, but you can't let your personal issues interfere with our business here. You have to follow the same ground rules as everybody else.'

"The manager went on to say, 'When she started to freeze up, I told her, 'You can't freeze up now. We have to be able to talk about your job performance. This isn't about your personal life. You can't use your personal life as an excuse for leaving early and then the next day tell me it's none of my business. You need to leave your personal issues at the door when you come to work. This is a place where you focus on work. You don't need to feel bad about your personal problems here. You can feel good about your work. Smile and use a pleasant tone of voice. Fake it if you have to. When you come in here, you have to be professional." To my total delight and surprise, she was fine after that—not that she didn't slip up now and then. My catchphrase with her after that was, 'Fake it if you have to.' That was my way of reminding her to be professional. I told her, 'I have to be able to talk to you about your performance without you freezing up. I have to be able to tell you when your performance is lagging and you need to improve. We have to be able to have these conversations.'"

The manager in Bruce Tulgan's story handled the employee and the situation well. But the point I want to make is to all the potential and current employees out there. Not all managers will be as tolerant or understanding. Part of how we are judged in our work has to do with our attitude. We might not always be able to change our circumstances, but we can adjust our attitude. Leave personal woes behind at the office door. Always maintain a professional demeanor and stay focused on producing the good work of which you are capable and a friendly, positive attitude with managers, coworkers and clients.

Finally, if interviewing with prospective employers, let that professional, positive, friendly attitude shine through!

About Bruce Tulgan

Bruce Tulgan of Rainmaker Thinking is an author and speaker. His bestseller, It's Okay to be the Boss, and his blog articles can be found at:
http://www.rainmakerthinking.com.

How To Say NO

How does one who is inclined to always say yes bring himself or herself to utter the big N-O with sugar on top?

Most of us don't like to disappoint others. When asked to be involved in something in which we're not particularly interested or when we have other plans, we often feel obligated to say yes. However, it's really okay to just say NO!

So, how does one who is inclined to always say yes bring himself or herself to kindly utter the big NO? My initial thoughts are:

- "Thank you for including me, but I'm unavailable."

- "Isn't that nice of you to ask? I'm sorry, but I won't be able to."

- "I appreciate your thinking of me. Please keep me in the loop."

- "No, I can't meet in person, but is there something you'd like to discuss?"

As an experienced businessperson of more than 40 years, it took me a long time to learn to say NO when I felt that involvement in a meeting or activity wasn't going to work for me. Even worse, young people today have so much stress put on them to be involved with multiple activities outside of work—all pressured by coworkers, family, friends and others. So let's look at some other ways to pronounce a well-mannered NO.

Here's a List to Use Next time you Need to Say NO to an Event:

- I would love to participate, but my schedule has reached critical mass, and I don't think I can do your project justice. Please check back with me, though, on your next one.

- Thank you for the invitation but I won't be able to make it this time. Please keep me in mind for the next event.

- Begin with a thank you or a compliment. "That sounds like a wonderful event" is always good, followed up with "and I'm sorry I won't/am not able to join you," etc. Don't use "but I'm sorry." The "but" often tends to negate the compliment. Don't go into great detail as to why you are saying no—a prior commitment, alternative plans, etc. It may be that you just want a quiet evening at home with a movie and popcorn; those are your plans and of no concern to anyone else. If you are pressed, repeat with a smile, "I simply have another commitment."

Other Ways to Say NO to Something about Which You Disagree:

- As much as I would like to agree with you . . .
- As good of an idea as it is . . .
- Even though I think it is a brilliant proposal . . .
- Even though I'm with you 90 percent on this . . .
- Good suggestion, but not what we're looking for at the moment.
- I'll take it under consideration and get back to you if it is a go.
- What a great idea, one we've considered, but . . .
- I'll take it under consideration.

Saying NO Face-to-Face:

If the invitation is in person and you are aware ahead of time that you are not able to participate, always look the person in the eye and preface what you are about to say with his or her name.

"John, that sounds great! I appreciate you thinking of me." Pause and then complete what you need to say. It may be something like this: "If I did not have plans, I would have liked to have come." Or, "John, it sounds interesting. Thank you. Let me look at my schedule and get back to you. What works best? Email or a phone call?"

If the invitation is over the phone, omit the eye contact. However, do preface your sentence with the person's name. Regardless of your preferences or how you are feeling at the time, treat the person with respect and gratitude. When speaking on the phone, it helps to have a good countenance. It comes through in the tone of your voice.

Special thanks to members of my LinkedIn Etiquette and Protocol Group for contributing these great ideas for this article!

Politics and Facebook

Oh, No, You Didn't Say That!

Back during the 2012 election week, Facebook became quite heated. During that time, I saw a thread on a political post made by one of my friends. The thread was about 20 comments long and got uglier as people added their thoughts, which became intentionally rude and disrespectful. It was all I could do to just keep scrolling. I've gotten in the middle of these discussions before, asking all parties to be respectful of each other's opinions, not to use profanity and certainly not to call each other names or belittle each other. It was like knocking my head against the wall. They all turned on me and started calling me names! I really believe that social media etiquette should be high on everyone's list as we go into any election.

I find this to be a true teaching moment. It's important for everyone, yes, but especially for teenagers and young adults, to learn how to discuss sensitive and inflammatory topics without resorting to profanity and insults that are aimed either at politicians and elected officials or at the people with whom they are discussing issues. This includes online comments on news articles and networking sites such as Facebook.

A fellow coaching friend recently shared with me that she recruited and trained college interns for a local political campaign. There were, of course, many political discussions among these mostly political science majors, and they were for the most part reasonable and respectful. There were occasions when someone would say something rude or off-color about the opponent or the opposing party, at which point she would remind everyone that they have an image to uphold, both for the campaign being represented as well as individually. They understood. The challenge occurred when a few disagreed with their own candidate's position on some issues and with members of the same campaign and political party. It was a learning experience for the interns to be able to discuss a subject on which they disagreed with respect for others' positions and opinions and with courtesy and restraint. Of course, being face-to-face is different than sitting behind your computer, since empathy and accountability are diminished.

Being "Unfriended" Because of Politics
A Pew Research study earlier this year revealed that about 18 percent of us "unfriended" somebody because of political posts put up on Facebook. Why? Because those posts often offend people in ways they do not even recognize. People have angered their bosses and offended their own families by posting political opinions. So, my best advice is just not to post political opinions, particularly in an excessive manner. If friends do post offensive statements, ignore them—don't respond. If you need to talk politics with them, do so in a face-to-face setting instead of on social media sites.

Maintain a Good Image

Here's another thought. It's important to constantly edit out images, messages and posts on your Facebook timeline that you feel don't reflect who you are. In other words, on Facebook, ignore bad behavior. Keep your own image just that . . . your own image. As the students in my friend's campaign training program learned to do, keep your own conduct and image as you would like to be perceived.

Remember, the rules of polite conversation DO apply to social media. Don't ignore that fact just because you don't have to look the person in the eye. As a rule of thumb, always say to yourself, "What would my boss or grandparents think if they saw this post?" Then go from there.

Some Simple Resolutions

Here are some simple suggestions for beginning any new year:

- Treat others with respect.

- Say thank you when someone does something nice for you.

- When making a request, use the word "please."

- Consider how your actions or words will affect others and then proceed accordingly.

- Don't make your life all about you. Try to help others. You'll be happier because of it.

- Consider that what goes around comes around.

- Perform simple acts of kindness for others.

ARE YOU GETTING THE PICTURE?

THE KEY CLASS

Life Has Changed

We Need Real-World Education

We have preschool to prepare us for kindergarten, kindergarten to set us up for first grade, elementary school to get us ready for middle school and middle school as a prerequisite for high school. But what is there to train us for life in the real world? The natural answer would be "our parents."

But Life Has Changed

Times were different when I was a youngster. Most mothers didn't work. Mine did, but my friends and I played outside unsupervised after school, on weekends and in the summer. Television wasn't a big thing, so we used our imagination, playing make believe, hiding from each other and making up games. Right at dusk, my friends would hear their mothers' voices and go home to wash up and sit with their families for their nightly semi-formal meal, where their parents would watch their table manners like hawks. Even though it was my job to make dinner when we lived in the ghetto, my mother always watched my brother and me as we ate our meal. Even when things got better for us, that never changed.

That's not as typical anymore. Did you know that there are approximately 13.7 million single parents in the

United States today, and that those parents are responsible for raising 21.8 million children (approximately 26 percent of children under 21 in the U.S. today)?[1] Even in a solid marriage, 64 percent of parents are dual-earners and 57 percent of them have children under the age of six.[2] Even with both parents rearing children, it is rare that they sit down for a meal around the dinner table on a nightly basis. Parents juggle both their work and, to compensate for their absence, a myriad of activities for the kids to stay active and learn good values.

Unfortunately, that doesn't always translate to good manners, respect or compassion. In a world that's "all about me," those things often fall along the wayside.

While my mother, after her hard day of work, focused on teaching my brother and me respect, good manners and how to treat other people, parents today are busy running to work, then running their children to activities, with little time for much else. In my time as a child, the focus wasn't so much on activities as it was on interaction. This doesn't mean that everyone isn't doing his or her best, but it supports a statistic from a survey of 3,000 business managers that 70 percent of people lose their jobs because they don't fit in.[3] Here, we go back to good manners, respect and how to treat others.

How to Get Real-World Education
How do we deal with it? The Key Class was created to teach people to truly survive in the real world—to teach them how to get and keep jobs that will be the mainstay of their livelihoods. This is critical to their success. This is also how adults can help themselves succeed in the real world. If you grew up in today's world, you may not have had the chance to gain the job-readiness skills that The Key Class teaches.

So, what should you do?

Go to www.thekeyclass.com and click on "Register for Classes Today" in the upper right corner. Courses run every Thursday for four consecutive, two-hour weekly classes. Pick a time block for yourself or your child. It will change a life.

---

1. United States. Census Department. Custodial Mothers and Fathers and Their Child Support: 2007. By Timothy S. Grall. Census, 2009. 26 Feb. 2010.
Eighty-four (84) percent of custodial parents are mothers, while 16 percent are fathers. And 79 percent of those mothers are gainfully employed while 90 percent of the fathers are as well. Forty-six (46) percent of them have two or more children living with them; 54 percent are raising one child.
2. United States Census Bureau, 2001.
3. www.careergeekblog.com.

They're Ignoring Us – What Can We Do about It?

I'm beginning to realize that not everyone can hold the attention of teens. I've been told, "It's futile. Just wait until they become adults, and then they will pay attention to what's important." I'm sorry, but I think that's baloney, and not the Oscar Mayer kind.

The other day, after teaching a class at the Santa Barbara County Probation Department, I got this note from Bob Foster of the Juvenile Institutions Office:

I was impressed with your presentation. Not everyone is able to hold the attention of a group like this. After 30 years in management, I must say that you impart a tremendous amount of good, usable information. For the next three weeks, may we bring in others even though they have missed the first session? If not we have the ability to provide other programming at another location. Thanks again.

We're talking about a group of teenagers who have broken the rules all their lives, and their teachers are trying to expose them to a different modus operandi so they can succeed, not fail. But they don't come into my classroom as willing participants. Can you picture a youth being dragged in by his hoodie? The rest of them enter and are so suspicious. "Why do we have to listen to this old guy? We know it all anyway!" You get the picture.

But I'm always prepared. I'm going to capture and hold the attention of teens learning something that doesn't make sense to them. Using good manners to get a job—seriously? No small trick. So how do I accomplish it?

Humor

First of all, humor will warm any crowd to you, and I use my wit with everything. Let's get real. Teens like to engage in things that are fun! So, I make it fun.

It's All about Them

I relate to them and their feelings. It's all about them, not me. Think about it. For teens, if it's not all about them, then they don't care about it! So I've got about 20 seconds to make them see that this isn't hoity-toity stuff, but that proper conduct in various life situations can get them the things they want. So I start with life situations to which they can relate. Take the guys, for instance. I tell them, "If you go out on a date with a girl, you don't show up wearing dirty clothes with dirty hair and fingernails. You don't want to show up all smelly. How do you think the girl would react to that?"

They laugh and volunteer something like, "Probably slam the door in my face!"

If I told them, "You must be groomed properly," they'd think, "Who the hell is this guy?" So it's imperative to talk their language.

Ask for Examples

I ask them all through class to give me examples. They don't like it at first, but by the end, they love it and are trying to impress the others with their examples. I ask the girls, "What things do guys do on dates that really aggravate you?" I get everything from "Paying more attention to their cell phones than me" to "Checking out other girls all the time." Then we talk about the negative outcomes of those actions.

Engage the Students who Get What I'm Teaching Immediately

One guy or girl in every class gets it right out of the gate, and I use that person as a straight man. They pick up on it and play back and forth with me. Everyone else then feels more comfortable.

For example, Robert sits in the very back row, his chair leaning against the wall. He closes his eyes and falls asleep just as I begin talking about body language. Ah, the perfect entrée! I call on him and ask him what he thinks about body language. The question rouses him, and he says he didn't hear what I said. "Robert, we're talking about body language and how we show whether we are interested or bored. I promise I'm not picking on you. But please, express to me how you'd feel if we switched places and you were teaching the class and I was sitting in the back row sleeping through it."

His chair falls forward, and he sits up. "I'd be insulted; probably angry. Maybe even feel like yelling at you."

I quietly ask, "How do you think I feel?"

Everyone laughs along with Robert, and the entire class sits up straight with him. Now I've got their attention.

Always Be on Their Level

I never let myself be better than them. I never mention it but make a huge point in my body language and actions.

Again, it's all about relating on their level. Having said that, I demand a certain respect.

Here's an example of what I mean. At a leading Santa Barbara high school recently, as I was speaking, a girl in the first class remarked, "Why the f@!# would you do that?" I said to myself, "I didn't hear that." After all, her teacher was sitting in the room!

Five minutes later, the girl next to her encroached on her space, and our little foul-mouthed beauty elbowed the intruder and said, "Move over, B#!#%." Again, I think, "Nawh, I must have misunderstood what she said."

Another 10 minutes goes by and she says f@!# again. Now I know I've heard it and immediately respond. "You know, I have to stop everybody. My favorite word in the world is f@!#, but you will never hear me use it, because I respect you and the relationship we have going here. It wouldn't be appropriate for me to use it in front of you, in public or with a client. There's a time and a place for everything."

I didn't look at her; I looked at everyone. I didn't embarrass her in front of everyone. I let her keep her dignity intact. And you know what? Never again did she say one foul word in my class.

My point? You guessed it: I'm relating to them. Once, a student referred to me as his "homeboy." My response? "Hey, buddy, I get it, but this isn't how you do this here and now." Nothing is different except there is a time and a place for everything. That's what etiquette is: following rules in different situations.

The Right Time and Place for Following the Rules

I let them know that I'm not the guy with the rules who's better than them. I let them know, "I'm the guy who wants to teach you the rules so you know when you break them!" And then, I tell them a personal story about me that is relatable to what they're going through.

I was a young designer, full of myself. I was unique, an individual, and I wore outrageous clothes, because that's what artists do! But I saw other people my age melding in better, becoming more businesslike, and it was working for them. So I decided I had to be a businessman and follow the rules to get ahead. With one of my first big presentations, I decided to try it out. It was with Delta Airlines, and I did research on how the company's corporate personnel dressed. Then I put on a nice suit and tie and tried to look like they did.

Being the passionate person I am, my presentation became quite exciting. I was waving my hands around (I know; I've coached you not to do this . . . but unfortunately, I do) and helping them imagine the event I would create for them. At one point, I asked if I could remove my coat, and not only did they tell me to do so, but they removed all of theirs as well!

When I went in, I looked as they did so they would trust me, and they did. If I had arrived dressed in a silk shirt, they wouldn't have listened to me because they couldn't have related to me. I looked like them, so they could talk to me. And, in the end, we all ended up without our coats (which made me feel more comfortable).

Show that It's All Right to Ask

Finally, it's important to know that most teens don't like to ask for anything. They're used to just taking what they want. The idea of asking is very difficult. So in order to teach them that it's all right to ask for help, I always say, "Are you willing to help me teach this class? I need your feedback because it is you I'm teaching!"

It's important for me to teach them to ask for the job when I'm teaching them job readiness skills. Numerous corporate executives who sit on various boards in which I participate often tell me that one of the biggest things people are lacking is that they don't ask for the job! They're lacking people like you to tell them what you want.

The Outcome
It comes down to this: relate to your audience by how you look, how you dress and what you say in words as well as body language. If you stay on your audience's level, whether they are teens or adults, they will respond positively to you, and success will be yours!

A Winning Formula

A Successful Partnership – The Key Class and Partners in Education

Partners in Education, a nonprofit organization active in the Santa Barbara community for more than 30 years, is on a mission to improve public education in a way that encourages a more vibrant economy and enriches the health of the community and the well-being of local children and their families. The organization is achieving its goal by connecting businesses and individuals with schools to partner and collaborate.

Partners in Education has Three Main Program Areas

• The Student Internships and Career Exploration Program – assists disadvantaged youth in finding their potential by arranging paid internship experiences with local businesses, as well as providing training in preparation for entering the workforce. The program provides six weeks of job readiness classes and eight weeks of paid work experience to sixty high school students each year.

• Computers for Families – an award-winning program that bridges the digital divide hindering low-income students from achieving academic success. This comprehensive program includes access to subsidized high-speed internet, training and ongoing technical support for teachers and families and a computer repair program at the Los Prietos Boys Camp. It serves more than 600 low-income students and families each year.

- Volunteer Recruitment and Coordination – recruits, trains and places community volunteers into local schools to prepare students for local jobs. An extensive database of volunteers is eager to help and can provide a broad scope of assistance, from mentoring to the arts, reading and tutoring to sports programs, interviewing techniques to job preparation, just to name a few.

A Successful Partnership
Through their mutual goals, Partners in Education and The Key Class have discovered a winning formula for success. John Daly, founder of The Key Class and board member for Partners in Education, has set up a comprehensive yet simple guide to business etiquette and life skills that gives participants the competitive edge to obtain jobs, advance in a current career or gain college entrance.

Daly and Partners for Education could see that students were struggling to make the transition from school to work, to secure jobs and to fit into the business world. Many students, as well as many adults, don't know how to succeed at work and life and lack self-confidence. Some don't know how to get along with or treat others with respect and lack concern for the world around them. Because of growing technology, the art of face-to-face interaction has often been lost and is apparent in the workplace. That's where The Key Class makes a difference.

What Do Key Class Participants Learn?
- How to make a great first impression

- The steps for a successful job search and interview process

- What is needed to start a business

- How to handle financial matters

- How to market oneself

- Dressing for success

- Table and meal etiquette during an interview or when out with the company's clients

- Building participants' self-confidence and concern for the world around them

- Making participants aware of their place in society and why it is important to earn and give respect

- Instilling accountability for one's own actions, which is a big plus for all communities

- Helping people understand how they can become valued members of business and society

The course is a series of lectures and discussions, consisting of four classes over four weeks, regarding a variety of business etiquette topics and how they apply to the workplace. Lecture and active discussion are combined with workshops, roleplaying, interactivity, games and fun.

What is Happening Now?

Daly started The Key Class in 2010 by teaching the course to at-risk teens through the Santa Barbara Teen Court, but he quickly expanded his program to multiple high schools in the county through Partners in Education. Their mutual plan is to expand to all high schools in the county in 2013. Through Partners in Education, The Key Class offers scholarships to students to participate.

To learn more about how you can help, please contact

John Daly at johnkeyclass@gmail.com, call 805-452-2747

or visit www.thekeyclass.com. For more information on

Partners in Education, please visit

http://www.sbceo.org/~partners/contact.html.

To read more about The Key Class, check out these links

on our blog:

http://www.thekeyclass.com/santa-barbara-county-teen-court/

http://www.thekeyclass.com/santa-barbara-independent-article-on-the-key-class/

http://www.thekeyclass.com/the-key-class-expands-to-santa-barbara-high-schools/

THE END

ABOUT THE AUTHOR

John Daly is an international legend in the world of special events. Known as the "Guru of Special Events Design," John is the founding owner and creative force behind one of the most successful event planning businesses in the world. Throughout his incredible career, he has studied the etiquette of a large variety of cultures, including those of Japan, France, Australia, South Africa, India and Korea, to name just a few. All these countries and more have hosted John to teach his field of expertise, and thus he began his hobby of understanding different societies worldwide. Soon, this hobby only added to the success of his event planning business.

His clients have included a full 25 percent of the Top 50 Fortune 100 companies, such as Gillette, MasterCard, Land Rover, Rolls Royce, Credit Suisse, Citicorp and Goldman Sachs, in addition to Hollywood entertainment companies such as KingWorld, CBS and Universal. He has worked for some of Hollywood's most well-known entertainers and celebrities, as well as others associated with the entertainment industry, including: Tom Cruise and Katie Holmes; David Beckham and his wife Victoria (Posh Spice); Will and Jada Smith; Oprah Winfrey;

Frank Sinatra; Bob Hope; and Dean Martin. He has created events for past U.S. Presidents, the State Department and the Smithsonian Institute. He designed and implemented the altar décor for ceremonies at The Los Angeles Coliseum and Dodger Stadium for Pope John Paul II's visit to the U.S. For many years he has been involved with World Cup Soccer and The Olympics, planning events surrounding their international festivities.

As an employer of many people throughout his illustrious career, John knows the importance of a positive interview process. His experiences interviewing, hiring and promoting his own staff, as well as working with top-level executives and celebrities, have taught him the importance of having the proper skills necessary to succeed. He attributes his training and social skills as the keys to his success.

In 2010, John began providing The Key Class to at-risk teens through the Teen Court in Santa Barbara County, California. It is his desire to expand The Key Class into a nationwide program, and he is working with local government agencies to begin to realize this goal. Working with Partners in Education in 2011, he piloted The Key Class to meet the needs of six high schools in Santa Barbara. As a result, he began teaching The Key Class in the majority of Santa Barbara County high schools in 2013. In addition, he is teaching in United Way's Fun in the Sun Program; at Boys' and Girls' Clubs; the Workforce Investment Bureau; and open classes on Thursday nights in Santa Barbara. His instruction doesn't end with the course. He then becomes a go-to person for any student to work on resumes, mock interviews or wardrobe selection.

His vision of a nationwide program encompasses classes not only for at-risk teens, but also for ESL students, high school, college and business school graduates, as well as returning veterans and job seekers, who also need this information to secure the right jobs and a brighter future.

CONTRIBUTORS

In Order of Contribution

8, 208-210
Andrea Michaels, President
Extraordinary Events
www.extraordinaryevents.net

28-31
Lydia Ramsey
Business Etiquette Expert/Speaker/Author
www.mannersthatsell.com

43

Northeastern University

43
Carol Kinsey Gorman
Forbes article, "10 Simple and Powerful Body
Language Tips for 2013

44
Amy Cuddy

http://www.youtube.com/watch?v=Ks-
_Mh1QhMc&feature=player_embedded

64-66
Pegotty Cooper, Speaker, Facilitator, Coach
Career Strategy Roadmap
http://careerstrategyroadmap.com/

65-66
Jeff Nelsen, Professor of Music, Coach, Speaker
Indiana University Jacobs School of Music and
Fearless Performance
https://www.facebook.com/FearlessPerformance?
fref=ts and
https://www.facebook.com/jeffnelsen?ref=ts&fref
=ts.

80-85
Lizandra Vega
Recruitment, Career and Image Expert, Author and
Blogger
http://www.lizandravega.com/about

86
George Bradt, Managing Director
Primegenesis
http://www.primegenesis.com/blog/our-executive-
onboarding-team/

96-99, 119
Terri Fowler
Professional Administrative Manager
http://www.linkedin.com/pub/terri-fowler/31/54/179

107-110, 138-140
Jeanne Nelson
Business Etiquette Consultant, Trainer, Speaker
and Former Administrative Professional
http://www.prowessworkshops.com/

114, 170-172
Deborah Choma, Associate and Instructor
Final Touch Finishing School
http://www.finaltouchschool.com/deborah.htm

115
Ruby Syring, Customer Relations and Specials
Events
The Boeing Company

115
Christine Chen, President
Global Professional Protocol
https://gpprotocol.com/

115
Teri Haynes, Owner
Business Interaction
http://www.businessinteractions.net/index.html

117
Mary Abbajay, Principal and Cofounder
Careerstone Group
http://www.careerstonegroup.com/

117
Protocol School of Washington

118
Catherine Albertini
The Etiquette and Protocol Institute of Rancho
Santa Fe
http://www.linkedin.com/pub/catherine-
albertini/b/1a8/954

118-119
Didi Lorillard
Newport Etiquette and Modern Manners
http://www.newportmanners.com/

119
Jay Remer
The Etiquette Guy
http://www.etiquetteguy.com/

120
April Ripley, Founder and CEO
Premier Image
http://thepremiereimage.com/credentials.html

131-133
Dan Janal, Author
Reporters Are Looking for You!
www.prleadsplus.com

134-135, 136
Rae Robinson
Freelance Writer
http://www.awaionline.com/bio/rae-robinson/

139-140, 211-213
Bruce Tulgan
Rainmaker Thinking, Inc.
http://www.rainmakerthinking.com

144
National Business Association
http://www.nationalbusiness.org/

150-151
Elena Neitlich, Owner
Etiquette Moms
http://www.etiquettemoms.com/

155
Peggy Post
Emily Post's Etiquette, 17th Edition
http://www.amazon.com/Emily-Posts-Etiquette-
Thumb-
Indexed/dp/B000GG4LSU/ref=sr_1_2?s=books&ie=
UTF8&qid=1360880284&sr=1-
2&keywords=Peggy+Post%27s+17th+Edition+of+Et
iquette

176-178
Monica Brandner, CEO
The Etiquette Princess
www.etiquetteprincess.com and
www.imagebymonica.com

191
Alixe Mattingly, Vice President, Communications
and Marketing
The Santa Barbara Foundation
http://www.sbfoundation.org/

199-202
John Wood
Freelance Writer
http://www.awaionline.com/bio/john-wood/

200, 203-207
Bob Burg
Speaker and Author
http://www.burg.com/

226
Bob Foster
Juvenile Institutions Officer
Santa Barbara County Probation Department

232-235
Santa Barbara Partners in Education
http://www.sbceo.org/~partners/